Endorsements

PRAISE FOR
THE ABUNDANCE PRINCIPLE

"*The Abundance Principle: Five Keys to Extraordinary Living by Jeff Standridge and Tim Kellerman is a book of great help to those of us who aspire to walk the spiritual path with practical feet. Don't miss it!*"

Ken Blanchard, Co-author,

The One Minute Manager® and *The Secret*

"*I highly recommend this book as a practical guidebook to lead you down the path of extraordinary living. Open the book, start reading now, and unleash the joy of* **The Abundance Principle** *in your life today!*"

Stan Toler, Author & Pastor

Oklahoma City, Oklahoma

D1510875

"In writing this highly readable spiritual guidebook, master teachers Jeff Standridge and Tim Kellerman have followed Jesus' example of presenting profound spiritual principles through simple stories that everyone could understand. Two thousand years later, Jesus' parables are quoted and repeated around the world. As **The Abundance Principle** circulates worldwide, these simple yet profound stories drawn from down-to-earth living will be repeated by believers who receive these blessings. I wish that 55 years ago, my wife and I had had this spiritual guidebook to teach us how to structure our new life together."

Dr. Dale R. Jordan, Author, Retired Professor, & Learning Expert

"**The Abundance Principle** is a brilliant reminder of the power of our own thoughts. More than that, it gives clear steps and actions that readers can implement to lead a truly extraordinary life. I've always believed there is enough to go around and this book proves it!"

Bradley Dugdale, Jr., Financial Consultant,
Author and Founder of the *Let's Save America Foundation*

"**The Abundance Principle** provides the practical tools you will need to create real wealth and live the abundant life God intended for you."

Monroe "Roey" Diefendorf, Jr., Author of "*3 Dimensional Wealth: A Radically Sane Perspective on Wealth Management*"

T H E
ABUNDANCE
PRINCIPLE

T H E
ABUNDANCE PRINCIPLE

Five Keys to Extraordinary Living

Jeff D. Standridge and Tim Kellerman

Published by
High Point Publishers, Inc.
813 Oak Street, Suite 10A-310
Conway, Arkansas 72032

In cooperation with
The Abundant Life Project™
http://www.AbundantLifeProject.com

Cover & Page Design
Maria Teeter Walker

The Abundant Life Project™ Life to the Full™ and *The Abundance Principle*™ are all trademarks of the Abundant Life Project.™

Library of Congress Control Number: 2006926332

ISBN: 0-9779340-7-1 (hard cover)
ISBN: 0-9779340-8-X (paperback)
ISBN: 0-9779340-9-8 (audio-book)

Printed in the United States of America

DEDICATION

Jeff D. Standridge: I owe a grand debt to my wonderful family. I have been blessed with a beautiful and loving wife and the best two children in the entire world. Lori, Katie, and Anna, you mean the world to me and I am so grateful to have you in my life.

I also had the good fortune of growing up in a loving home where laughter was frequent. Mom, Dad, Michael, & Angela thank you for your love and friendship throughout the years. I love you all.

In loving memory:
Calvert & Gladys Grant and
Dr. George Wayne Martin

Tim Kellerman: After 22 years of marriage, I have seen the words in this book lived out in vibrant color through the lady I call my wife. Jamie, you have brought abundance to me in so many ways. You are the love of my life. Sarah and Seth, what sheer joy you give to me. I love you dearly. Just so you don't forget, your attitude will always determine your altitude.

Dad, Mom, and Cindy: Thank you for my Christian heritage. You gave me everything I needed to make it in life and ministry. I am so proud of you. I love you.

Finally, I owe a debt of gratitude to my second family: the congregation and staff of the First Church of the Nazarene in Conway, Arkansas. Thank you for your investment into my life and my family.

ACKNOWLEDGMENTS

Anytime a work like this is undertaken, there is a multitude of people who make it happen. There is a special team of people who have helped us tremendously beginning on day one. This team worked hard to create and launch a website to support our efforts and we would be completely remiss without expressing our sincere thanks to Kaay Burris, Betsy Domingue, Stefanie Wilson, & Guss Riddles. Guss continues to work with us in an ongoing manner and we don't know what we would do without him. He has such a willing spirit and we are so grateful for his friendship, for his assistance, and for his personal ministry.

We also owe a great debt of gratitude to the reviewers who agreed to give us feedback on the book – John Bemis, Ken Blanchard, Kent Britton, Leisa Davis, Marilyn Davis, Jim Davidson, Roey Diefendorf, Jr., Bradley Dugdale, Rodney Engeler, Susan & Mark Freedle, Jim Garlow, Greg Gough, David Grant, Brenda Gray, John Hamon, Dr. Dale R. Jordan, Jamie Kellerman, Phillip Kellerman, Bob Lynch, Ann Martin, Connie Marvel, Angela & Shawn Moss, Rev. Charles Murry, David Nelson, Gary Pate, Todd Richardson, Bari & Mike Sells, Lori Standridge, Ina & James Standridge, Kristie & Chris Smith, Meredith & Scott Thone, Stan Toler, James Lee Whitt and Debbie Young.

Finally, we would like to express a special word of thanks to our cover designer and layout artist – Maria Walker, and to Pete Hoelscher for his invaluable editorial support.

Authors' Note: We have written this book in prayerful consideration and close collaboration with each other. Some of the experiences described are clearly individual, personal experiences. In those instances we have made an attempt to identify the writer. However, in order to make it less confusing for the reader, we have chosen to primarily use a unified voice.

In addition, we place ourselves in the "target audience" for this book. As the authors, we are writing about these concepts for our intended readers. However, we are also writing to ourselves. All of us are in need of reminders about these simple, yet profound concepts. For this reason, you will find the pronouns "we" and "our" used quite extensively.

CONTENTS

Foreword

When Jesus said, "I have come that you might have life and have it more abundantly," He meant it. The key is discovering how to live out everything those words mean. That is the gift that Jeff and Tim give to us in this book. You will not want to miss a single word.

In this book we have been given practical handles on how to embrace and apply **The Abundance Principle** in our lives through the Five Keys to Extraordinary Living. Frankly, the keys themselves are extraordinary. But, Jeff and Tim present them in a fresh and dynamic way that it seems as if they are "right out of the box."

We know that it is only through Jesus Christ that we can receive the abundance He spoke about in John 10:10. However, what the authors do for us is help us see that there are a few choices we make along the way which can dramatically increase the degree of "abundance" we experience throughout our lives.

I love the way Jeff and Tim remind the reader that living properly often depends on thinking properly – choosing a thought pattern that leads toward rather than away from abundance. They also discuss the calling of God on our lives. The authors demonstrate that to experience extraordinary living, we must discover our purpose, and then arrange our lives such that we are able to pursue that purpose.

Relationships are an essential part of our lives. Jeff and Tim remind us that we were all created for relationship. Since this is such a significant part of living, it is vital that we make good choices in how we relate to others – both friend and foe alike.

Finances can be a controlling factor in our lives. In fact, money is often the trigger to conflict in marriage and family. However, it is also the catalyst to many good things in life. Choosing to handle our money well is essential. The authors give practical advice to move us toward financial abundance without teaching a prosperity gospel.

Generosity is a choice. If life is gift-wrapped it only makes sense that it is meant to be given away for the benefit of others. Jeff and Tim show us the impact of giving & serving for the good of others.

I highly recommend this book as a practical guidebook to lead you down the path of extraordinary living. Open the book, start reading now, and unleash the joy of **The Abundance Principle** in your life today!

Stan Toler, Author & Pastor
Oklahoma City, Oklahoma

Introduction

"An unexamined life is not worth the living."

Socrates

Have you ever moved to a new house and had to pack up everything you owned? Did it amaze you how quickly you accumulated all of that "stuff?" Many of us even trade our stuff for other people's stuff. Jeff once traded a guitar he never learned to play for an automatic bread-making machine. His friend wanted to learn to play the guitar and Jeff wanted fresh, homemade bread. It was a match made in heaven.

Some people make a living traveling around on Saturday mornings from yard sale to yard sale, buying other people's stuff and selling it in their own flea markets and garage sales! It certainly validates the saying, "One man's junk is another man's treasure."

Have you ever stopped to think about how much stuff you actually do have? We have more phones than we have televisions. We have more televisions than we have Bibles. We often throw away more food than we eat. We spend money on things we never wear. Face it … we have an abundance of stuff. Some might even say we live "abundant" lives … that is, on the outside.

Our hearts, however, tell a different story. Emotional disorders and depression are at an all-time high. One out of every two marriages ends in divorce. Seventy percent of marriages report significant financial difficulties. Our friendships are shallow. We break promises to ourselves and to others. Sometimes we feel trapped in the "rat-race" of life, running from place to place, doing the same thing day after day, wondering if life will ever improve, or worse yet, if it will ever end.

> *"Until the pain of remaining the same is greater than the pain of change, people will choose to remain the same."*
>
> Anonymous

Currently, the population of the world stands at almost six and one-half billion people. We are told approximately 32% are categorized as Christians – that's more than 2 billion people. It is our conviction that if 2 billion of the world's population were completely committed to Extraordinary Living, the world as we know it would be a radically different place.

If we were all committed to Extraordinary Living, the world as we know it would be a radically different place.

We hear about better ways of living in countless numbers of sermons and motivational speeches and we read about it in books day after day; we assent with our minds and declare agreement with our lips. Yet a vast number of us drive away from churches every Sunday in expensive SUVs to elaborate homes totally devoid of the personal fulfillment that ought to be ours – that can be ours.

According to research firm The Barna Group, when comparing social issues, Christians mirror non-Christians in divorce, addictions, domestic abuse, and financial difficulties, among a host of other things. Christians struggle with addiction. Christian marriages are in trouble. Christians spend themselves deeply into debt. Christians take a host of medication for ailments and illnesses brought about by excessive stress, anxiety and depression, all of which the Bible says we can have victory over through Christ. Somewhere there is a "disconnect" between what God's Word says is ours, and what we actually experience. The fact is most of us have more than any other generation in terms of material goods. Yet statistics, current events, and daily headlines reveal a less fulfilled people today than ever before.

We have some good news to share with you. We can experience life as abundantly on the inside as we appear to be experiencing it on the outside. We can live extraordinary lives. This is what the Abundant Life Project™ (www.AbundantLifeProject.com) is all about. It's about reclaiming a privilege belonging to every person on the face of the planet: The right and freedom to live an extraordinary life. We want to spread the word: Extraordinary Living can be the experience of everyone.

Somewhere there is a "disconnect" between what God's Word says is ours and what we actually experience.

In this book, we introduce you to five simple concepts we call the Five Keys to Extraordinary Living. As you'll see, Extraordinary Living is the kind of living from which abundance flows – but not just in terms of material things. We're talking about abundance in every major area of our lives.

We believe we do not decide our future. We decide our habits and our habits determine our future. From this point forward, your future is full of hope, fulfillment, and unlimited possibilities. You only have to develop the right habits.

The Abundance Principle: Five Keys to Extraordinary Living is your guidebook to developing those new habits. It is organized in a manner to help you take advantage of the Five Keys as you progress through the book. Take your time. Read slowly and thoughtfully. Take notes in the margins. Underline key passages that seem to resonate with you. At the end of each chapter you'll find two critical elements – Key Points and Key Actions. Carefully review the Key Points and, by all means, thoughtfully and faithfully complete the Key Actions as well. It is in reading, reflecting, thinking, praying and then doing that we begin to change our lives for the better. If we fail to take action, we're left with the same debilitating habits that restrict us to lives of weakness, insignificance, and sometimes despair.

We do not decide our future. We decide our habits and our habits determine our future.

Now before proceeding, as the authors, let us be the first to say … we have NOT arrived at our final destinations personally. We, too, remain completely susceptible to the ups and downs of life. We're still "works in progress" ourselves. However, we try to wake up every day and pursue extraordinary living with vigilance. And as we consciously and persistently pursue this type of living, we're finding it a little less elusive along the way. We're convinced you'll find the same.

CHAPTER ONE

A Chronic Condition

"Nothing is enough for the man to whom enough is too little."

Epicurus

A chronic condition displays itself in thousands of airports across the globe on a daily basis. Perhaps you've seen it. You're sitting at the gate with several dozen other people. You have a boarding pass in hand for a specific seat, to which no one else is assigned. You know the customary practice is for the flight attendant to open the doors to the gate and announce the boarding process. Normally, the attendant begins with travelers who need special assistance, followed by first and business class passengers, and then economy class passengers … boarding from the rear forward. It's a fairly simple and standard process. Most of us have done it at least once or twice.

However, this chronic condition to which we are referring becomes readily apparent at the precise moment two or more people anticipate the flight attendant is about to open the doors to the gate. When the first anticipatory movement is made by two or more awaiting passengers, the stampede begins. People immediately begin crowding the boarding area even though they know precisely when they'll be called upon to board, and precisely where they'll be sitting when they do board.

This condition also shows its face in family buffet lines at restaurants. At some point in life, most of us have developed this perspective that there's not enough to go around; so we should get all we can. As a result, masses of people crowd the buffet lines, filling their plates to overflowing in order to ensure their own appetites are satisfied before the buffet table gets scavenged by other diners.

We see this condition again during income tax season. As we try to maximize the tax refund we'll receive, we're sometimes tempted to "stretch" the rules just a bit. We'll claim a little extra mileage to the doctor, or perhaps overestimate the value of the bags of clothes we dropped off at Goodwill. We might even mislabel an expense or two as legitimate business expenses, even though they clearly weren't.

It is especially clear on Sunday mornings as the offering plate passes us by. Have you ever noticed how small a $20 bill seems at the grocery store, and how huge it seems on Sunday mornings? We freely give up money for expendable items we want or need today

Have you ever noticed how small a $20 bill seems at the grocery story and how huge it seems on Sunday morning?

and can't even remember buying tomorrow. But when it comes to following through with consistent and generous planned giving to our Church or favorite charity, we find a multitude of reasons why we "can't afford it."

Finally, it appears in the workplace in more ways than we can count. It's visible when we take office supplies home for personal use.

It's visible in the win-lose negotiations of a major deal. And it's visible in the competition among employees for honor, recognition, and praise.

This chronic condition – sometimes called "the Scarcity Mentality" – is living life to get all you can before someone else beats you to it. It's hoarding the resources we have out of fear we might not have enough to live the lifestyle to which we've become accustomed. It's maximizing our own benefit, regardless of how doing so might disadvantage someone else. The end result of the Scarcity Mentality is a life "on the take."

THE SCARCITY MENTALITY

Stephen Covey first introduced us to the scarcity mentality in the late 1980s in his highly acclaimed book *The Seven Habits of Highly Effective People*. According to Covey, scarcity-thinking springs from a basic innate belief that the human and natural resources existing in the world are too limited to allow all of us to achieve our goals and realize our dreams. It operates from a self-centered basis of insecurity and competition, suggesting life is a zero sum game – meaning, when one person wins, that success is perfectly balanced with the loss or failure of someone else. Also called win-lose thinking, a person with this belief pattern sees the world as a pie of very specific and finite proportions. There's only so much to go around and if you get more, that means I get less. If you get a bigger slice, that means my slice will be smaller.

In the summer of 2005, the Gulf Coast of the United States suffered a devastating hurricane season. Specifically, the coast along

Mississippi, Louisiana, and parts of Alabama was hit particularly hard. In the immediate aftermath of the storm, many of us watched in horror the news footage from New Orleans where people of all ages were looting stores, carting away tons of computers, televisions, and the like. Forget the fact that many of these same people had lost homes, cars, family members, etc. The Scarcity Mentality took over and it was time to go get stuff ... before someone else got it first.

Hundreds of thousands of people were displaced, some permanently, by the devastating storms. The opportunity arose to help a specific lady who arrived in our city from New Orleans. She and her family were part of the several thousand people who could not be evacuated before the storm, and who were subsequently moved to the New Orleans Convention Center. This lady, in her sixties, was a diabetic and in fair health at the time of the storm. She survived six days with no food and was eventually evacuated to a hospital in our town.

The Scarcity Mentality – Living life to get all you can before someone else beats you to it.

It was completely shocking to hear her describe her experiences after the storm and the flooding. She explained that the strong people at the convention center were eating 5 and 6 meals a day, while the weak ones were denied food. Those too weak to stand up for themselves were literally pushed away from the table by a few of the strong ones. The Scarcity Mentality was definitely at work in New Orleans during that time.

Most of us probably first experienced the Scarcity Mentality as children, but didn't even realize it. Early on, children develop a very a clear expectation that everything within reach belongs to them. Regardless of whether they're carrying a piece of candy, a toy, a bowl from the kitchen, or a pillow, a single attempt to take it away is clearly and demonstrably rebutted with shouts of "Mine!" If you've ever had a two-year-old, you know full well the reason God makes them to be little people is to keep them from taking over the world.

One of the first fables we learn as children is that of the "Goose that Laid the Golden Eggs." In this story, a poor farmer discovers that one of his geese lays golden eggs. Of course he is delighted with this surprise finding; however, as his wealth begins to grow he becomes somewhat impatient with the pace of golden egg-laying. This goose lays only a single egg each day.

As his greed and impatience finally overcome him, the farmer kills the goose, cutting it open in hopes of getting all of the gold at once. Of course we know that in doing so this man destroys not only the goose, but his wealth-building capability as well. The farmer's Scarcity Mentality gets in the way of his continued financial success.

Early on, children develop a very clear expectation that everything within reach belongs to them.

We even see evidence of the Scarcity Mentality in the Bible. Take the story of brothers Jacob and Esau. Prior to the death of a father, it was customary for him to give his blessing to the firstborn son. When their father Isaac became old and ill, he was unable to see well and told his firstborn, Esau, to go and hunt wild game to prepare a meal for him so that he could then grant his blessing. Having overheard this, Rebekah – Isaac's wife and the mother of Jacob and Esau – devised a scheme to deceive Isaac and obtain the blessing for her favorite son Jacob instead of Esau. Jacob disguised himself by wearing Esau's clothing and after successfully deceiving Isaac, he was able to steal away the blessing that was intended for his older brother Esau. Both

Rebekah and Jacob were victims of a clear win-lose mindset. For Jacob to win, Esau had to lose.

Another biblical example is that of Moses and Aaron. After they led the Israelites out of Egypt, the people were grumbling about the conditions in the desert and especially the lack of food. God gave very clear instructions that he would "rain down" bread for them each morning and would give them quail to eat each evening. Their instructions were to go out and gather only the amount of bread they needed for that day. They were clearly instructed NOT to hoard or to keep any bread through the night because a fresh supply would be provided the next morning.

Nevertheless, many people succumbed to the scarcity mindset and kept portions of their food beyond the evening time. When they awoke in the morning, the bread was spoiled, full of maggots and smelled badly. All they had to do was gather bread in the morning and quail in the evening and dispose of any uneaten food prior to retiring for the evening. Yet the tendency to embrace the Scarcity Mentality appeared to be stronger than their faith in what God had told them.

Approximately 70% of all divorce cases report having financial difficulties.

Jesus spoke to us about the Scarcity Mentality in the twelfth chapter of Luke as He tells a story called "The Parable of the Rich Fool." In this story, a certain rich man had very fertile ground that produced a bumper crop. The crop was so large that the man did not have room to contain it. He decided to tear down his barns and replace them with larger ones. Once the new barns were completed, his harvest would provide for him for years to come. His plan then was to sit back and take life easy; to "eat, drink and be merry." However, Jesus issued a stern warning; "… Watch out! Be on your guard for all types of greed; a man's life does not consist in the abundance of his possessions."

Here is a very rich man caught up in clear-cut scarcity thinking. His intention was to hoard his supply, quit working, and live the good life. Scripture goes on to tell us that while he was planning his future, everything was taken from him, including his life. Hoarding and greed are based in the scarcity mindset, as demonstrated by this rich fool from Jesus' story.

MORE THOUGHTS ON SCARCITY-THINKING TODAY

The effects of win-lose thinking are also clearly visible today, both in the face of tragedy, like the New Orleans example, and in everyday life. Our society has become so accustomed to the effects of scarcity-thinking that it's sometimes difficult to trace the event back to its cause.

We all remember not long ago when corporate scandals seemed to be the norm. Large, well-known companies were caught "cooking the books" by using creative accounting techniques to report higher profits than those actually achieved. This practice, of bending the truth, whether done in large corporations, in small home-based businesses, or on personal tax returns, is an indication of the scarcity mentality at work.

Crimes of violence and dishonesty are clearly a result of the Scarcity Mentality. Can I get something for nothing? Can I win regardless of how badly someone else has to lose? As a result, we have a litany of crimes that fill up the law books in order to define and explain every possible way someone might commit crimes of scarcity (such as burglary, mugging, robbery, embezzlement, extortion, murder, rape, and so on).

There is a classic story about the death of an extremely wealthy man who lived a lavish lifestyle. As you can imagine, his funeral was a very grand occasion. According to his specific request, he was not buried in a coffin. Rather, he was seated in his huge Cadillac limousine, dressed in a black tuxedo, with a cigar in his mouth. During the graveside service the entire car was lowered into the grave. One bystander was heard to have remarked, "Man, now that is really living." That's a funny story, but also a truly sad commentary as well. Unfortunately, the Scarcity Mentality has a tendency to follow us all the way to the grave, robbing us of our joy in the here and now.

These examples are obvious evidence of a scarcity obsession that seems to pervade our society. But could it be that there are more subtle examples of this mindset at work in your lives on a daily basis? Could it be that you frequently fall victim to this chronic condition of life yourself? Answer these questions (yes/no) to see if it's possible that the Scarcity Mentality has a hold on you as well:

1. When clearly undercharged by a cashier or when I am given too much change after a purchase, I always correct the cashier even if it will end up costing me more money.

2. When preparing my Income Tax Return, I only take deductions for which I am clearly entitled and always have the proper documentation to substantiate the deduction.

3. When a co-worker, spouse, sibling or friend receives a promotion or special recognition for a job well done, I am always very happy for them and demonstrate that happiness without reservation.

4. When approaching an on-ramp while driving down an interstate highway, I routinely move into the left-hand lane, or at least slow down, in order to allow vehicles on the on-ramp to merge successfully.

5. When I have a meal at an "all-you-can-eat" buffet, I only fill my plate with that which I know I can eat, and I resist the urge to over-indulge.

Did you see yourself in any of those questions? If you answered "No" to any question, then like us, you experience the Scarcity Mentality on occasion as well.

At the time of this writing, it is the morning of Thanksgiving. Sales flyers fill the newspapers. Commercials litter the television shows. The holiday shopping season begins tomorrow. In fact, two days ago at a local retail outlet, a line had already begun forming to get a coupon for the latest and greatest video game on the market. It was about 2:00 p.m. and the coupons weren't even being handed out until 10:00 p.m. But the line had already formed. On the Friday after Thanksgiving, people will get up earlier than they do most workdays and flood the retail stores in hopes of getting a jump on their holiday shopping before all of the good items are gone. In fact, one of the greatest marketing ploys used by the makers of toys and leisure devices is to actually cultivate the Scarcity Mentality leading up to the Holiday Season. If they can succeed in making the buyers think that the desired item is in scarce supply or will be otherwise tough to get, demand will definitely increase!

You've never seen a hearse with a luggage rack, and you'll likely never see one pulling a U-Haul.

29

It's important to note that the Scarcity Mentality is no respecter of persons. At one time or another it affects us all. And, it's inward turmoil has an obvious outward manifestation. It shows in our behavior, in our faces, and in our countenance. A story is told about a little girl who visited her grandmother in the country. This lady attended a very old-fashioned church that kept very strict rules for what could and what could not be done on Sundays. In fact, they forbade all work, fun, levity, laughing and/or playing. The little girl awoke on Sunday morning and commenced doing what little girls do. She started playing and laughing. Her grandmother immediately scolded her for breaking the rules regarding Sunday activities.

Later that day after attending church, the little girl went for a walk out by the barn. She walked over to an old droopy-eyed, sad-faced, long-eared mule. After looking at the mule for a few moments she said, "Mr. Mule, you look like you go to my grandmother's church!" Much like that old mule (and the members of Grandma's church), our outward expressions tend to indicate our inward turmoil.

PRISON-THINKING

A variation on scarcity-thinking is what has been referred to as "prison-thinking." It's the type of thinking that says, "It's not fair," or "Why me?" The term was used by Captain Charlie Plumb, a former Naval Aviator who flew the F-4 Phantom jet on 74 successful combat missions over North Vietnam. On his 75th mission, just five days prior to his return home, he was shot down over Hanoi and parachuted into enemy territory. He spent the next 2,103 days (six years) in an 8x8 foot communist prison cell. Thanks to another

American prisoner in the cell next to Captain Plumb, through their secret conversations across the cell wall, Charlie was able to identify and ultimately overcome his prison-thinking.

Prison-thinking is a belief that tells us we have no power over the circumstances we face or our response to those circumstances. Author and trainer W. Gary Gore further describes this belief pattern:

"It is also known as 'victim-thinking' or 'stinking-thinking' and directs us to see ourselves as pitiable, whining, little bundles of human flesh buffeted to and fro by an environment over which we have no control. This kind of thinking is endemic in our society today and most of us spend our time making excuses and blaming others for why we cannot do something."

Prison-thinking is a crippling force that robs us of our capabilities and achievements. It's the thinking that prevents us from taking appropriate risks, from launching that new business, forming that new friendship, going back to school, or just enjoying life. While it's not a physical prison cell with concrete walls and steel bars, it is very much an emotional prison. And it holds us captive by our fear, our anxiety, and/or our scarcity thinking.

The point is that we all experience the Scarcity Mentality or we all have instances of prison-thinking, probably on a daily basis. It's that little voice in the back of our heads saying, "You better hurry," or "You better get a little more pie before it's gone," or even "It's not my fault!" It exists in all of us, but as we'll see in the chapters

Prison-thinking tells us we have no power over the circumstances we face or our responses to them.

that follow, it prevents us from living an extraordinary life. In order to improve our living, we must improve our perspective. We must overcome the Scarcity Mentality and other forms of win-lose thinking.

A CHRONIC CONDITION – THE SCARCITY MENTALITY

KEY POINTS

- "The Scarcity Mentality": Get all you can before someone else beats you to it.

- Scarcity-thinking: There's not enough to go around. If I get more, you get less. If I win, you lose.

- Everyone is susceptible to the Scarcity Mentality.

- A variation on scarcity-thinking is what has been referred to as "prison-thinking." It's the type of thinking that says, "It's not fair," or "It's not my fault!" The tendency of the prison-thinker is to immediately place blame.

- Prison-thinking is a belief that we have no power over the circumstances we face or our response to those circumstances.

- Prison-thinking is a crippling force that robs us of our capabilities and achievements.

- To improve our perspective and improve our lives, we must overcome the scarcity mentality and other forms of win-lose thinking.

KEY ACTIONS

- Write a short (one page or less) narrative describing yourself. Start the narrative with the words, "I am ..." Be honest. If necessary, go back to the short "self-test" in this chapter and use those questions to get you started.

- Create a list of words or phrases you commonly use and describe how you use them. Ask for feedback from someone you trust and with whom you are close (friend, parent, spouse, sibling, etc.).

- Spend some time reflecting on this narrative. Make an overall judgment about the points you like and dislike about yourself. Create two short lists containing the things you like and dislike about yourself, as described in this narrative.

- Examine the areas of your life that seem to cause you the most personal turmoil or stress. Take a long, hard, and honest look to see if you are caught up in the habit of "prison-thinking." If you find that you are, list 3-5 things you can do now to change that habit.

"I cannot always control what goes on outside. But I can always control what goes on inside."

Wayne Dyer

CHAPTER TWO

A Better Way of Living

*"When one door closes another door opens; but we so often look
so long and so regretfully upon the closed door, that we do not see
the ones which open for us."*
Alexander Graham Bell (1847 – 1922)

A few years ago, I (Jeff) had the opportunity to travel with my family to Kosovo on a mission trip. We stayed with a local family who lived in a two bedroom, one bath house of approximately 700 square feet. Living in the house were six adults and four children, ranging in age from eighteen months to seven years.

The entire family lived on the equivalent of approximately $600 per month. The grandparents earned about half of that monthly income by teaching in the local village school where they had been teachers for the past 35 years. The remaining income was earned in the family "street market" where they sold bread, vegetables, canned goods, and other items.

Just three years earlier, this family had lost everything they owned.

Because they were ethnic Albanians, living amongst racially-provoked Serbians, they were driven from their home, forced to walk three days to the Albanian border, only to be turned back upon their arrival. The Grandfather and the eldest son were both imprisoned in Serbian prison camps, leaving the women and children to fend for themselves.

To hear stories of what they and other similar families suffered under the tyranny of Slobodan Milosevic prior to the NATO intervention was heart & gut-wrenching. Most Kosovar-Albanians were sorely mistreated, robbed, deprived of food and other basic necessities, and sometimes beaten. This particular family slept in fields during the day, and moved around to forage for food and other necessities at night. If anyone had the right or reason to develop a bitter outlook on the world – to employ "prison-thinking" – it would be this family and a host of others in Kosovo. However, they set the example for a completely different mindset.

From the moment we stepped into their home we were treated like long-lost friends and family. During our stay of approximately two weeks, the entire family moved into a 10x12 - foot space under the house, used an outdoor bathroom, and allowed us to sleep in their beds. They cooked our meals, did our laundry, and in other ways treated us almost like royalty for the entire duration of our stay.

The entire family moved into a 10x12 – foot space under the house and allowed us to sleep in their beds.

Every day they greeted us with smiles, hugs and laughter. They acted as though they had been truly blessed for their entire lives and only wanted to share with us a portion of the blessings they had received. On more than one occasion during our stay, I asked myself who was on a mission to help whom.

During dinner, on the night before our departure, we were surprised by an outpouring of generosity. This precious family, as well as others in the village, gave us gifts! Every person in this family lived from a perspective of abundance rather than scarcity. They never allowed themselves to become victims of prison-thinking. The love and care they showed for us superseded their concern about money or comfort.

Similarly, several years ago, I (Tim) saw specific examples of "abundance-thinking" as well, and I didn't even realize it at the time. My wife and I led a group of young people into the interior of Mexico to do light construction and conduct Vacation Bible School for the children from the mountains. For a week we made a little town named Matlapa our home. As we interacted with those simple people, I saw something that changed me forever.

I saw people who had very little. I saw people living in extreme poverty by my standards – grass huts, dirt floors, open fires as ovens, and pots filled with dirty water for washing. I saw people who wore clothes that were obviously second hand – clothes that had been discarded as out of style by American standards but good enough for these people.

I witnessed a way of life that was hard. One young boy named Timothy, who was about 10 or 11, carried a 5-gallon container on his back which he filled once or twice daily with water from a creek and carried to his primitive home. Clothes were washed by being beaten on a large rock near a running stream. Miles of travel was required to acquire even the most basic necessities of life and most often was conducted on foot.

What I called less than adequate, these kind and gentle people called everyday life – and they seemed strangely content with that life.

At the time, I simply wrote it off as a case of "you can't miss what you've never had." But as I began to explore what it is that brings contentment to our lives, my mind went back to our friends in Matlapa. They had only a fraction of what I had in terms of material goods, but they seemed to have it all in terms of peace and contentment. I spent some time thinking about what I had physically seen with my eyes. Then, I began looking at them with the eyes of my heart. Suddenly, I saw something completely different.

I saw peace in their eyes, love in their hearts, joy in their smiles, and contentment in their demeanor. It wasn't until I was back home, surrounded by my "stuff" that it registered in my mind what they really possessed. What I saw but didn't realize at the time was authenticity. It wasn't forced. There were no masks and certainly no pretense. I was seeing the real thing – real people, completely content with their surroundings, not chasing after some artificial or temporal goal. And every time I think about them, there is a pull in my heart to have that. And I would be willing to give up some of what I have to get it.

They had only a fraction of what I had in terms of material goods, but they seemed to have it all in terms of peace and contentment.

If you've ever traveled to a third-world country, or a country of significantly lesser means, you've witnessed the fact that many people who live outside modernized countries are often more joyful, more content, more loving, and more giving than those of us who have everything. They seem to be much happier, while at the same time possessing significantly less then we who live in the land of plenty. Their provisions and possessions might be scarce, but everything they do is real. Often their perspectives, demeanors, attitudes, and actions spring from an abundance mindset. How can that be? We believe the absence, or at least the reduced influence of commercialism and TV sensationalism, has allowed them to grow up with the reality that abundance is not what you have, it is who you are.

THE ABUNDANCE MENTALITY

[1] Opposite the Scarcity Mentality which sees the world as a finite pie with limited amounts for everyone, the Abundance Mentality sees the world as a plentiful place of unlimited abundance. Abundance-thinking recognizes that there is plenty enough to go around and that there is no need to scramble for "stuff," or hoard things for the future. In addition, the Abundance Mentality sees the world as an infinite sea of possibilities and opportunities. It springs from a strong sense of self-worth, personal contentment, and peace.

From where does this different way of thinking come? Could it be possible that the peace and contentment experienced by our friends in these two examples is available to everyone regardless of their race, face, or place? According to Jesus, we can be certain that it is.

Perhaps you are aware of the promise of eternal life found in the Scriptures, in John 3:16. But few recognize that according to Jesus, He also came to give us "abundant" life in the here and now.

In the tenth chapter of John, Jesus intertwines his discussion about providing the way to salvation with the thought about living an abundant life.

"The thief comes not but for to steal and to kill and destroy; I have come that you might have life and that you might have it more abundantly."

John 10:10 (KJV)

In contrast to the thief who takes life, Jesus tells us that He is the giver of life. The life He gives, however, is abundantly richer and fuller than the life we try to live on our own. Life lived according to the guidance of Christ is life lived on a higher plane. The mission of Jesus is that we might have life, and that we might have it "more abundantly."

To understand the impact of this mission statement, it is important that we come to a better understanding of the word "abundance." Most dictionary references for "abundance" will say something about "more than enough," "plentiful" or "bountiful." A quick search through several different translations of Scripture finds the use of synonyms such as "wealth," "plenty," and even "safety."

The phrase "more abundantly" is a relative phrase. According to Jesus, we can live life "more abundantly" tomorrow than we are living it today. If we are living in the gutter today it's easy to picture a "more abundant" tomorrow. But even if we are living well today, Jesus' message to us is the same: There is a better way. We can begin experiencing an even better life ... a life that is "more abundant" than anything we've ever known.

Abundance-thinking recognizes there is plenty enough to go around and there's no need to scramble for "stuff."

When we read the same Bible passage from the New International Version (NIV), the phrase "more abundantly" is translated "to the full." This phrase is a bit more descriptive. In it, we learn a little more of what Jesus is actually talking about. "Life to the full" is still a relative phrase, but it's not relative to how we're experiencing life today. It's relative to our capacity to experience life. Experiencing life better tomorrow than we are experiencing it today is certainly a good and noble thing. But experiencing it at full capacity is even better.

Now, this is where our study of the phrase "more abundantly" gets really good. If we dig just a little deeper, we see that the original word used is "perissos." Looking at all possible meanings of this term we uncover statements like the following:

- Exceeding some number, measure, rank or need

- Over and above; more than is necessary; superadded

- Exceeding abundantly; supremely

- Superior; extraordinary; surpassing; uncommon

If we take at face value the actual intended meaning regarding what Jesus came to do, we see that He came that we might have life "beyond full capacity." It's over the top. One particular definition or synonym gives us the full impact of this perspective – superadded. That is what Jesus came to infuse into our lives. Not only can we live life to the full, we can get "over full," a life that has been "superadded" to. The mission of Jesus is that we might experience life over and above our normal capacity. He changed our capacity, increased it, and made it possible to experience life on a completely different level.

> *"You prepare a table for me in the presence of my enemies. You anoint my head with oil, my cup overflows. Surely goodness and love will follow me all the days of my life, and I will dwell in the house of the Lord forever.*
>
> Psalm 23: 5-6

41

BIBLICAL EXAMPLES OF THE ABUNDANCE MENTALITY

Throughout the Bible we see clear evidence that the Judeo-Christian God is a God of abundance, not scarcity. In the passage from John 10:10, Jesus is telling us that living life with God at the center is a life of abundance.

All the way back in Genesis we see that God created man and woman in His image to live abundant lives. Before the Fall of Man, Adam and Eve lived in The Garden of Eden. God gave them everything He had already created and told them:

"Be fruitful and increase in number; fill the earth and subdue it. Rule over the fish of the sea and the birds of the air and over every living creature that moves on the ground."

Genesis 1: 28

God created us, starting with Adam and Eve, to live abundant lives. The prophet Jeremiah also spoke of God's intentions regarding His people after they had been forced into exile from Jerusalem to Babylon.

"... seek the peace and prosperity of the city to which I have carried you into exile. Pray to the Lord for it, because if it prospers, you too will prosper ... For I know the plans I have for you, declares the Lord, plans to prosper you and not to harm you, plans to give you hope and a future."

Jeremiah 29: 7 & 11

God tells us in the first chapter of Jeremiah that He knew us while we were still in the womb. He went on to say in this passage that His intention was to give us hope, a future, and prosperity. What more could we wish for? God's intention for us is that we will have divine hope, a divine future, and divine prosperity ... now that's something to get excited about. God told Jeremiah that he intended for us, His people, to live extraordinary lives!

In the 66th chapter of Psalms we come to another reference regarding God's abundance. It is important to note that the anonymous author has just won a great victory in battle. His entire psalm is a tribute to God for the guidance, protection, & mercy He has shown:

"You let men ride over our heads, we went through fire and water, but you brought us to a place of abundance."

Psalm 66:12

The psalmist is saying, "We experienced tough times ... really tough times, but when we put our trust in God, He brought us out to a place of abundance."

THE ABUNDANCE PRINCIPLE REVEALED

In Luke 12, Jesus teaches about worry – another common symptom of the Scarcity Mentality. The basis of his lesson on worry is the common fear we all face about whether we have enough "stuff" to be comfortable. He explains that even the birds and the lilies have everything they need to live comfortably and then He gives us a glimpse of *"The Abundance Principle."*

"Do not be afraid, little flock, for your Father has been pleased to give you the kingdom."

In essence, Jesus is simply reiterating the fact that God's plan, since creation, has been that we will live abundant lives. Previous Scripture already points to this fact, but Jesus proclaims it again in this passage. He then goes on to tell us in John 10:10 that it is His *personal* mission to see that we experience it: *"I have come that you might have life and that you might have it more abundantly."* There it is. We call it ***"The Abundance Principle."*** Write it down if you have to. Carve it in the stone tablets of your mind, because it's at the core of Extraordinary Living.

———————

The Abundance Principle
An abundant life has been God's plan for us from the very beginning.

———————

God created us in *His image* to live abundant lives. As we've seen, numerous stories throughout the Bible remind us of how God frequently rescues us from our own self-absorbed, self-created struggles, and brings us out to a place of abundance. His intention for us from the very beginning was that we would live our lives in abundance.

EXTRAORDINARY LIVING IS ABUNDANT LIVING

So what does it mean to live an extraordinary life? First of all, we believe Extraordinary Living is Abundant Living. Our previous study of the phrase "more abundantly" certainly supports this belief. But what does Extraordinary Living look like? Would someone know if I were living an extraordinary life? Would I know it? All too often we pursue things in our lives that we can't even define or describe. In our minds, however, we would describe Extraordinary Living as certainly having at least some of the following characteristics:

God created us in His image to live abundant lives.

- To work extremely hard on something and watch someone else enjoy it;

- To follow through on a difficult job until it is finished;

- To endure an injustice without becoming sour on the world;

- To use balanced criticism to improve yourself and to accept unfair criticism without letting it beat you down;

- To carry out an act of kindness when the easiest thing is to do nothing;

- To carry money in your pocket without spending it;

- To willingly help those in need without thinking about what it's going to cost you;

- To do what's right when no one else is watching;

- To know your God-given purpose and to pursue it with passion;

- To have peace of mind and soundness of heart because you know you've given your best to God and to others;

- To be thankful for God's abundance even when, by the world's standards, you may have very little;

> *"To laugh often and love much, to win the respect of intelligent people and the affection of children, to earn the approval of honest critics and endure the betrayal of false friends, to appreciate beauty, to give of one's self, to leave the world a bit better, whether by a healthy child, a garden patch, or a redeemed social condition, to have played and laughed with enthusiasm and sung with exultation, to know even one life has breathed easier because you have lived ... This is to have succeeded."*
>
> Ralph Waldo Emerson

What a great way to live. Can you imagine the changes that would occur in the world if everyone pursued that type of living?

In a nutshell, Extraordinary Living is about experiencing the sustained, heartfelt joy that is generated when we have a healthy command of our thoughts and mental processes; when we have a clear and articulate purpose for living and we pursue it with passion; when we have many friends and very few enemies; when we have a reasonable degree of financial security; and when we truly give of our heart, our hands, and our money for the glory of God and the good of others. At the end of the day, it is about living well on the outside, but it's also about knowing and feeling on the inside that we're living well. That is the definition of Extraordinary Living.

GETTING THERE

But how do we get there? How do we learn to live extraordinarily?

A semi truck, apparently hauling fine furniture, provides a possible answer. In bold letters underneath the company name is emblazoned this catchy phrase: "Fine furniture begins on the inside!" The same thing can be said of Extraordinary Living ... it begins on the inside! The battle for abundance begins within us.

Someone along the line has declared that we are our own worst enemy. If we could just catch up with ourselves we could win a few more life battles – especially the battle for abundance.

So, what are the circumstances that stand in the way of our achieving abundance? Right up front we have to become honest with ourselves. It will be impossible to engage the thoughts and actions that lead to Extraordinary Living until we conduct a serious and honest inspection of who we really are

Extraordinary Living begins on the inside.

and what is really going on inside of us and around us. This is not a concept that we can jump over and ignore. The path to abundance begins right where we are.

While we cannot control all of the difficult circumstances we face, the important things are ultimately within our control. The decision of whether or not to take control of them is simply a choice we make. In the words of pastor and author Chuck Swindoll, "Life is 10 percent what happens to us and 90 percent how we choose to react to it."

Perhaps the first step to Extraordinary Living is found in the words of Professor Howard Hendricks, you must "overthrow the stale and sterile government of your thinking." That is where the first key to Extraordinary Living begins.

A BETTER WAY OF LIVING – THE ABUNDANCE MENTALITY

KEY POINTS

- The happiest people are those who learn that abundance is not what you have. It is who you are.

- The Abundance Mentality arises from a strong sense of self-worth, personal security, and peace.

- Jesus said He is the giver of life in contrast to the thief who takes it away. The life He gives is abundantly richer and fuller than the life we try to live on our own.

- The mission of Jesus is that we might have life, and that we might have it "more abundantly."

- "More abundantly" means "beyond full capacity" or "over full."

- *The Abundance Principle* states that an Abundant Life has been God's plan for us from the beginning. He created us in *his image* to live abundant lives.

- Abundant Living is Extraordinary Living.

- Extraordinary Living is the outward translation of an inward abundance. In John 10:10, Jesus tells us that inward abundance is a result of living life with God at the center of our lives.

- While we cannot control all of the life circumstances we face, we can definitely control our responses to them.

- Extraordinary Living requires us to "overthrow the stale and sterile government of our thinking."

KEY ACTIONS

- Review the short narrative you wrote about yourself after Chapter 1. Use your understanding of the Abundance Mentality to review your narrative, as well as the "likes" and "dislikes" list. Make revisions where necessary in order to ensure the narrative and the lists most accurately reflect who you are currently.

- Make a written list of everything for which you are or should be thankful. Include all of the blessings and other positive things in your life. Take your time in creating this list. Pray that God will reveal all of the things for which you should feel gratitude and record them all on your list. Spend time reviewing this list in an effort to gain a healthy perspective regarding just how blessed you really are.

- Develop a habit of starting each day by cultivating the genuine emotion of gratitude toward God for your many blessings. This can be assisted by reviewing your list or by reading key passages of Scripture dealing with God's blessings or in other ways you may find useful (i.e. Psalm 23).

"The world we have created is
a product of our thinking;
it cannot be changed
without changing our thinking."

Albert Einstein

As a Man Thinks

"The greatest discovery of my generation is that a human being can alter his life by altering his attitude of mind."

William James (1842 -1910)

On a hot sultry day in blue skies over Negev, Israel, two F-15s and four A-4N Skyhawks were engaged in a simulated dogfight. At some point the F-15 collided with one of the Skyhawks. Initially the pilot of the F-15 thought the huge strike he felt was caused by passing through the jet stream of one of the other aircraft. Before he could react, however, the pilot saw a big ball of fire created by the explosion of the Skyhawk.

The radio delivered the message that the Skyhawk pilot had ejected. Suddenly the pilot of the F-15 understood that the hit he felt was the Skyhawk which had exploded, and that the pilot had been ejected automatically. As fuel streamed out of the wing of the F-15, it dawned on the pilot that the impact with the SkyHawk had sheered off a wing of his own aircraft.

The aircraft went into an out of control, downward spiral causing the instructor pilot sitting in the rear position to issue the order to eject. Instinctively the pilot switched off the autopilot and took the controls. Slowly, he regained power of the aircraft until it was straight and level again. The pilot later said, "It was clear to me that I had to eject. But when I gained control I said; 'Hey, wait, don't eject yet!'"

Since the wing is a fuel tank, and the fuel indicator showed "empty," the pilot assumed that the jet stream had sucked all the fuel out of the other tanks. However, he thought he might have enough fuel to get to the nearest airfield to land, so he began a quick descent.

The pilot worked like a machine. He wasn't scared and didn't worry. His training in emergency procedures was fully engaged. He made a lightening-fast decision: As long as the plane was in the air, he was going to stay inside.

He started to decrease the airspeed, but at that point one wing was not sufficient. The plane immediately went into a spin down and to the right. A second before ejection was absolutely essential, the pilot pushed the throttle and lit the afterburner. He regained speed and subsequently, control of the aircraft. The next thing he did was to lower the arresting hook and call the tower to erect the emergency recovery net. A few seconds later the plane touched the runway at 260 knots, about twice the normal landing speed.

> *"All that a man achieves and all that he fails to achieve is a direct result of his own thoughts."*
> James Allen (1864-1912)

The hook was torn away from the plane fuselage because of the high speed, but the aircraft managed to stop 10 meters before the net. When the pilot turned back to shake the hand of his instructor, who had previously urged him to eject, he saw the damage for the first time. He had actually flown and landed a plane with only one wing! Sheer determination, training, and probably most importantly, his mental and emotional toughness had literally allowed the pilot to defy incredible odds, including the Law of Gravity, to successfully land his aircraft.

MIND OVER MATTER

As we have already discussed, God has created in us and around us everything we need to live extraordinary lives. However, because of the scarcity mentality, many fall short of the prize of living life to the full. As we begin to think of what it will take for us to rise above our circumstances and live the way God intended for us to live, it is a logical choice to begin with our minds. The Apostle Paul gave some

> *God has created in us and around us everything we need to live extraordinary lives.*

good advice and strong council to the believers in Rome when he said, *"Do not be conformed to this world but be transformed by the renewing of your mind"* (Romans 12:2).

As we attempt to navigate through life in extraordinary fashion, our thinking will often travel against the grain of current culture. Like the F-15 instructor pilot, there will be people or circumstances around or behind us who will shout into our ears, "eject, eject, eject." In these times we will be tempted to conform to the standards of society. But, if we let God renew our minds, as the Apostle Paul advised, we will experience such transformation that even if we are flying against the winds of popular culture, we will make a successful landing. And what constitutes a successful landing? Paul completes

> "Live your beliefs
> and you can turn the
> world around."
> Henry David Thoreau

verse 2 with the answer: *"…that you may prove what the will of God is, that which is good and acceptable and perfect."* A renewed mind – one that is able to perceive what God believes to be good, acceptable, and perfect is the beginning of understanding abundance.

CULTIVATING OUR MINDS

Our minds are like gardens. In order for a garden to be optimally fruitful, it must be cultivated and nurtured. There must be adequate moisture and sunshine, in addition to appropriate nutrients. As author James Allen suggested, regardless of the care taken by the gardener, all gardens ultimately bear some type of fruit. If no useful effort or seeds are put into the garden, the fruit will end up as useless weeds, spreading throughout the garden like wildfire. However, if the gardener dutifully cares for and cultivates the ground, keeping it free from weeds, the intended flowers and fruits will flourish and grow in abundance.

The same is true of our minds. If we allow the Master Gardener to cultivate our minds, like an earthly gardener cultivates the soil, He will weed out all of the wrong, useless, and impure thoughts, so the flowers and fruits of right, useful, success oriented thinking can abound.

Our role in this, however, should not be underestimated. We have to take the responsibility of choosing to think differently. Once we make that choice, we prepare the ground for the Master Gardener to begin His work.

On the journey to Extraordinary Living, the mind is indeed a key component. In fact, it may very well be the primary key. Our thoughts and beliefs about God, others, ourselves, our circumstances, and our future are critical to whether or not we will ultimately succeed in life. It is for this reason that we suggest the first key to unlocking the power of **The Abundance Principle** is as follows:

Master your thoughts and change your life.

In 1992, I (Tim) suffered what I now know as an anxiety attack. While driving home from a meeting, my heart suddenly started racing uncontrollably. My breathing felt like it was being choked off. I literally thought I was going to die. From that moment and for the next 2 years, I entered a depression that consumed my life. Only my wife knew. As I look back, I cannot imagine the darkness my life brought to her. She was helpless – helpless to understand what I was going through – helpless to guide me through the darkness.

What seemed to wrap me the tightest, what sent me spiraling into a near debilitating sorrow, was an overwhelming fear of death. Why, I don't know. This fear of dying would wash over my body without warning like a tidal wave. It was unpredictable. It would happen in the car, in the shower, in my office. My life became filled with the negative, the fearful, and the sorrowful.

On Sundays I would preach the good news to a receptive congregation. I spent the remaining six days each week trying to find what I told my congregation was available to them.

A few years ago a popular movie came out about a man on death row. It was entitled *Dead Man Walking*. That is how I would describe where I was during that period in my life. Every waking moment I dealt with death and dying and what that would mean for my family. I was slowly dying on the inside. I needed to be transformed. For me, it was a life or death matter.

Time and time again I prayed that God would heal my mind of this terrible battle waging within me. At one particularly low time, when it seemed I could no longer bear the internal turmoil, I pleaded again for God to deliver me from the terrible darkness that cloaked my life. I sensed, for the first time, that God was giving me direction. That divine guidance would change my life forever. It seemed so simple, yet for me it was powerful. I was impressed with the tremendous truth that if healing was going to take place in my life, I had to change the way I was thinking. The New Living Translation of Romans 12:2 explains well what I knew must happen within me:

Don't copy the behavior and customs of this world, but let God transform you into a new person by changing the way you think. Then you will know what God wants you to do, and you will know how good and pleasing and perfect his will really is.

Romans 12:2 (NLT)

There it was. With God's help I had to change the way I was thinking. If I had any hope of a normal life, I had to let the Master Gardener re-cultivate my mind. It was time to replace the negative with the positive – but not just any positive. I had to practice what I preached. I began to memorize hope-giving Scripture. I began to fill my mind with God's Word. Some days I would quote the same Scripture over and over again like a broken record. I saw this as the only remedy for my condition. My favorite passage became, *"I can do everything through him who gives me strength."* (Philippians 4:13).

Slowly but surely things began to change. The episodes of darkness became fewer and fewer. Light was returning to my life as I forced out the negative with positive, hope-giving scripture and thinking. It has been 14 years since that day occurred. I am happy to say since taking control of what went into my mind, God has removed the darkness and I have not experienced an anxiety attack since.

Filling my mind with the positive, affirming words of Scripture directly affected the thoughts that consumed my life. Literally, what was happening on the inside directly affected the way I thought outwardly. However, mastering my mind meant controlling what went in. It meant changing what I thought. It was a choice ... a choice of which I seized control.

Perhaps you've heard the story about an old granddad who was napping on the couch. As a prank, one of his visiting grandsons lightly rubbed blue cheese into the bushy mustache under the old man's generous nose. An hour or so later the elderly gentleman awoke. Immediately he sensed a sour odor in the air. Sniffing around, he wandered around the house trying to find the source of the odor. In the living room he said, "The living rooms stinks." In the bedroom he said, "The bedroom stinks." In the kitchen he said the same thing. Finally Granddad went out onto the porch. Lifting his face to the sky he inhaled a lungful of air through his nose. "Good grief," he said, "the whole world stinks."

> *Mastering my mind meant changing what I allowed inside it.*

Too often we let the circumstances of our life dictate "how the world smells." While we know that many terrible things can happen to us, we make the choice whether or not we let those things fill our lives. In Ephesians 3:19 Paul prayed that his readers might be "filled with all the fullness of God." This is the whole goal of the Christian life and a very important point for extraordinary living.

The word "filled" generates the idea of being dominated by something. If you are filled with rage, then rage will dominate your life. If you are filled with love, love dominates your life. A person filled with gratitude lives a life that is dominated by gratitude. When you are filled with God, then God Himself will dominate your life. The same holds true for our minds. When your mind is filled with good things, good things dominate your mind. Perhaps it is for this reason that the Apostle Paul declared:

" ... *whatever is true, whatever is noble, whatever is right, whatever is pure, whatever is lovely, whatever is admirable – if anything is excellent or praiseworthy – think about such things."*

Philippians 4: 8

Why would Paul give such advice? It could be that he understood that the way we think not only affects us and how we live our lives, but also affects the people around us.

CHANGING WHAT YOU THINK CHANGES
THE WAY YOU THINK

The first step in mastering your thoughts is simply to change what you allow yourself to think. This in turn changes the way you think, which leads to a more positive and constructive way of living.

Our perspective has much to do with how we feel. Most of us believe the way we feel is determined by events completely outside of us. We tend to think that as something happens to or around us our emotional state automatically changes in response to that event. In reality, our emotional state changes, not due to an event itself, but because of what we think about that event. In other words,

Too often we let our circumstances dictate "how the world smells."

from moment to moment, we create our own feelings and emotional states by allowing ourselves to think certain thoughts.

World-class athletes develop a habit of managing their thought processes leading up to a major competition. They don't simply train for years leading up to the Olympics and then "hope" they feel great on the day of the actual event. They train their minds to convince their bodies that they feel great. They control what they think in order to manage how they feel.

Author and master trainer T. Harv Eker, as well as speaker & trainer Bob Proctor, teach a very important concept using The Process (The Law) of Manifestation, which can be expressed in the following formula:

$$T + F + A = R$$

This formula explains that our thoughts (T) lead to our feelings (F), which in turn drives our actions (A). The results (R) we achieve come about because of the actions we choose to take. Results tend to drive new thoughts, and the progression repeats itself. When we understand this natural progression of thoughts, feelings, actions, and results, we become more aware of how much of our own results we actually influence and possibly even control in our lives.

MAINTAINING A POSITIVE PERSPECTIVE

Reframing a particular event or set of circumstances is a great technique for changing the way you think and subsequently feel about that particular event. By reframing a negative event into a positive outcome, we not only change the way that event makes us feel in the here and now, but we also increase the likelihood that a similar set of circumstances in the future will end more positively.

> *"We're not retreating, we're advancing in another direction."*
> General George S. Patton

I'm reminded of a great story about a small boy who was pretending to be a professional baseball player. He affirmed, "I'm the greatest batter in the world," after which he tossed the ball in the air and took a swing as it descended. "Strike One!" Before tossing the ball in the air a second time, he again affirmed, "I'm the greatest batter in the world." Again, the boy swung at the ball as it rapidly descended. "Strike Two!" A third time the boy stated, "I'm the greatest batter in the world," and tossed the ball in the air for the third time. Once again the boy swung and missed. "Strike Three!" As he gathered up his glove, baseball and bat and headed for home he said to himself, "Well how about that, I'm the greatest pitcher in the world."

Disciplining ourselves to maintain a positive perspective is one of the best ways to manage our thought processes. Author Napoleon Hill said that every adversity brings with it the "seed of an equivalent benefit." By this he means that problems are also opportunities in disguise. There is no such thing as failure, only feedback. This feedback, if viewed and used constructively, can provide us critical information to eventually find success. However, without a positive perspective and the recognition that we have the ability to adjust our tactics to overcome the present circumstances, this negative feedback defeats us, leaving us to wallow in the finality of our failure.

Make it a habit to look for the "seed of an equivalent benefit" in every negative circumstance or situation you face. You may not find it quickly in every case, but you will open your mind to a number of possibilities that will take the focus off the circumstance itself. In the end, you'll discover that you have more power over the situation than you ever thought possible.

EXPECTING THE BEST

Often we are completely unaware of our underlying attitudes. We walk around subconsciously expecting the worse. Do not be mistaken. Though we are not always aware of our negative outlook, we have a choice every single day as to what attitude we will embrace. We can all change our lives for the better, but to do so, it is absolutely essential that we change our attitudes.

As we've discussed, the emotional response we experience to any given situation is a product of our underlying beliefs and how we think about that experience. Many times we get caught up in a cycle of blaming others

Disciplining ourselves to maintain a positive perspective is one of the best ways to manage our thought processes.

and refuse to accept any responsibility whatsoever for the circumstances of our lives. We claim we had bad parents, bad teachers, a broken home, a terrible employer, an unfortunate accident, etc. We closely follow those claims with a denial of any personal responsibility.

We quickly protest, claim that life isn't fair, and point the proverbial finger at someone or something else. As a result, we come to expect bad things and guess what? Our expectations are met ... bad things happen. When we take complete and total responsibility for our lives, we make the incredible leap from being a child to being an adult. Letting our circumstances determine our emotions is a surefire recipe for a life of disappointment.

> *"Action and feeling go together; and by regulating the action, which is under the direct control of the will, we can indirectly regulate the feeling, which is not.*
> William James

Consider this: Dante's *Divine Comedy* originated as a result of watching a boiling cauldron of smelly tar. William Booth conceived the idea for the Salvation Army as he walked through a reeking and hopeless-looking slum in 19th century London. Lewis Carroll is said to have designed much of his *Alice in Wonderland* while suffering from migraine headaches. Meanwhile, stories abound of athletes, business men and women, teachers, ministers, etc., who came from virtually hopeless backgrounds, but overcame severe adversity to achieve great things in life.

People who tend to succeed in their endeavors take total and complete responsibility for their lives. They have a positive perspective and this perspective determines their ultimate expectations. If we expect success, regardless of our endeavor, and we believe we are taking steps that will move us toward success, then we take positive actions that increase the likelihood we will experience positive outcomes. If however, our attitude is negative or we believe (even subconsciously) that we will fail, we will interpret everything that happens to us as a validation of that belief.

AVOIDING THE BLAME GAME

We live in an age of victims. Litigation is at an all time high. People everywhere want to get even. They want to blame someone else for their misfortune. The recent tragedies surrounding the hurricanes that pounded the Gulf Coast is a good example. It was only a few hours into the recovery process when people started pointing fingers of blame for the levy disasters in New Orleans. Without question, there is probably someone to blame. However, who to blame is still in question. The ones doing the blaming are obvious.

If there is one thing that can prevent us from Extraordinary Living, it is being shackled by bitterness, resentment and blame. So much mental and emotional energy is expended on defensiveness, self-righteousness, revenge and vindication that nothing is left for any productive output. The truth of the matter is that the only one suffering from this silent battle going on inside us is ... well, us.

> *"A noble and Godlike character is not a thing of favor or chance, but is the natural result of continued effort in right thinking, the effect of long-cherished association with Godlike thoughts. An ignoble and bestial character, by the same process, is the result of the continued harboring of groveling thoughts."*
>
> James Allen

Most of us have probably heard the analogy that holding a grudge against someone is like drinking poison ourselves and expecting the other person to die. In fact, it's been said that a man who refuses to forgive destroys the bridge over which he himself must one day cross.

Let us help you take a major step toward Extraordinary Living right now. Are you ready? Here it is. It is actually the title of a song sung by the Eagles in the early 90s. *"Get Over It!"*

Now, before you shut the book and discard it with yesterday's newspaper, let us clarify something. To *"Get Over It!"* means to take control of the situation. You see, a particular situation or circumstance may very well be someone else's fault. And it may be completely and totally unfair. As the saying goes, "Life ain't always a bed of roses." But if you don't get over it and move on, it then becomes your fault. While there may be people out there who are responsible for some of the negative circumstances of our lives, it becomes OUR responsibility to determine the ultimate outcome … the end result. WE make the choice as to whether a bad situation will make us bitter or better. We cannot be a victim and a victor at the same time. It just can't be done. We're either one or the other. Extraordinary Living is about claiming victory regardless of the circumstances.

For some, "getting over it" may mean seeking the assistance of a counselor, psychologist, or pastor. If that is the case, by all means seek it out.

With that said, let us add this word of guidance. For some, "getting over it" is no easy task. It can mean changing a life-time of negative thinking about someone or something. What you have to "get over" may in fact be so traumatic and painful that you will need the assistance of a professional counselor, psychologist or pastor. If that is the case, by all means seek it out. Taking control of the situation means being proactive … even if it means asking someone else for help. Don't allow something or someone to control what you think or believe. When we expect the best we are better able to stand up and claim victory regardless of the situation or circumstance.

WITH WHOM ARE YOU THINKING?

Let's be honest. We don't always do our own thinking. The reality is we were not born with our attitudes and thought patterns. We acquired them from our parents, our friends and the world around us. Most of our thought processes have been conditioned by the significant people in our lives. While many of those people have played positive roles shaping our thinking, there are some who have had a negative impact on us. Some people have been emotionally crippled because of certain significant others in their lives. The truth is that how we think as adults is how we were taught to think as children.

The result is that we can become paranoid, skeptical, critical, and negative. If we are not careful, that thinking can become a part of the fabric of our lives, affecting everything about us including our relationships, our careers, our financial success, and our personal fulfillment.

The reality is, we were not born with our attitudes and thought patterns. We acquired them from our parents, our friends and the world around us.

We have already said that to begin mastering our thoughts, we have to control what we think, the way we think, and the tendency to let people or circumstances think for us. In order to successfully master our thoughts, we might also have to change the people with whom we are thinking or interacting.

Someone once said, "You can't soar with the eagles when you're scratching around with the turkeys." How true that is. Have you ever been around someone who can walk into a room and simultaneously drain all the positive energy out of the air? Some people can be so negative and critical that if we spend too much time around them, we can begin to act like them ourselves. It happens all the time with children. Just place your young toddler in a room with other toddlers who are whiney, spoiled and openly defiant and see what happens. If you are a parent, you know what happens. As quickly as the time it takes to strap your child in the car seat and head for home, your child will begin to see what he can get away with. He will test you. He will see if whining works. He will see if arguing works. He will see if manipulation is effective. Last but not least is the out and out defiance. He will push until he discovers where the boundaries are. If you don't clearly reveal the boundaries, he will extend them. How did all this happen? All it took was spending a couple hours with another child who was out of control.

The same thing happens to young people. The same thing happens to adults. Spend time with a happy person, and inevitably you will become happier yourself. Spend time with a sad person, and they will drag you down. Spend time with a negative person, and if you are not careful, the things coming out of your mouth will be a result of what you have been taking into your mind. Garbage in, garbage out ... isn't that the saying?

We must learn to challenge the underlying expectations and assumptions we hold in life. We must learn to separate what happens to us in the circumstances of life from who we are as a person. We must remain in control of our attitudes. If we are to live Extraordinary Lives, we must regain control of our minds and think for ourselves. But we must do so in a manner that leads to positive outcomes. Master your thoughts and you are guaranteed to change your life for the better.

> *"There is no such thing as bad weather, only the wrong clothes."*
> Billy Connolly

THE FIRST KEY TO EXTRAORDINARY LIVING –
"MASTER YOUR THOUGHTS AND CHANGE YOUR LIFE"

KEY POINTS

- James Allen compared our minds to a garden. If we carefully cultivate our mind and weed out all of the wrong, useless, and impure thoughts, then the flowers and fruits of right, useful, success-driving thinking will abound.

- The mind may very well be the primary component in the journey to extraordinary living. How we think about God, others, ourselves, our circumstances, and our future is critical to whether or not we succeed in life.

- Mastering our minds means controlling what goes in. It means changing what we think. It is a choice … a choice of which we must take control.

- Mastering our minds often begins with mastering our attitudes.

- WE make the choice whether a bad situation will make us bitter or better. We cannot be a victim and a victor at the same time. We are either one or the other. Extraordinary Living is about being a victor.

- In order to successfully master your thoughts, you might have to change who you are thinking (interacting) with. "You can't soar with eagles when you're scratching around with the turkeys."

KEY ACTIONS

- Sit down with a pad of paper and a pen and take an inventory of what you regularly put into your mind. What do you talk about with your friends and family? What do you read? What do you watch on television? What do you listen to in your car? Be very specific. Closely examine this list and identify the positive things versus the negative things. Reflect on your findings.

- Make a commitment to fast from "negativity" for a minimum of 30 days. Refuse to read or watch horrific news stories. Refuse to listen to talk-radio shows or TV stations that only engage in political debate. Tune your car radio to a positive or inspirational radio station or insert an inspirational CD or audiotape into your car stereo. Visit the "Related Links" at www.AbundantLifeProject.com to locate a positive and encouraging radio station in your area.

- List the commonly held beliefs you have about yourself in the following areas. Your Looks; Your Intelligence; Your Talents and Skills; Your Capabilities; (Are they generally positive or negative?)

- Download a copy of *The Abundance Principle Thought Planner* from www.AbundantLifeProject.com and complete it.

- Pick a particular passage of Scripture or favorite reading (try Philippians 4:8) that captures the benefit of positive, healthy thinking and commit to reading it at least three times a day for the next thirty days. Read it early in the morning, read it during the middle of the day, and read it at night.

CHAPTER FOUR

A Clear Direction

"Things which matter most must never be at the mercy of things which matter least."

Goethe

Back in the hill country of the south, the story is told of two brothers who hired a pilot to fly them to Canada to hunt for moose. After a couple of days of hunting, the pair bagged their limit of six moose and summoned the pilot for their return flight home. Upon surveying their cargo, the pilot quickly informed them that the plane could not handle the entire load. In fact, he explained that the top-end limit for the plane was four moose.

The two hunters from the south objected strongly. "Last year we killed six moose and the pilot let us bring them all home. He had the exact same plane as yours." Reluctantly, the pilot relented and allowed the hunters to bring all six moose with them.

Unfortunately, even at full throttle, the load was just too much for the plane and it went down shortly after take-off. Climbing out of the carnage of the wreck, one of the hunters asked the other, "Any idea where we are?" To which the other hunter replied, "Yeah, I think we're pretty close to where we crashed last year."

Although a bit ridiculous, that story strikes a chord at the heart of humanity. How many times have you done something in the exact same manner as you had done it previously, but fully expected to get a different result? Unfortunately for many of us, it's something that happens before we realize it and unexpectedly we feel completely embarrassed afterward.

It is not uncommon for people to look up at age 40, 50, or even 60 and wonder, "Where has my life gone?" or "Why have I not done any thing significant yet?" Perhaps they've charted a clear-cut course

> "A man without a goal is
> like a ship without a rudder."
> Thomas Carlyle

for earthly, career and/or financial success, but then seem surprised when they fail to achieve real significance. They've been doing the same thing every day for many years, but somehow expecting their lives to arrive at a place called "Significance." They chart no course to Significance. They make no plans for how they will get there, but nonetheless, they have this underlying expectation they will get there.

In the early 1900s Andrew Carnegie, the founder of a predecessor company to US Steel, commissioned a young attorney and journalist with what ended up being his life's work. This young man, Napoleon Hill, would spend the next 20 years assembling and analyzing the qualities that directly contributed to the success of the great persons of that time. All in all, he would interview more than 500 titans of science, business and government including Henry Ford, Thomas Edison, Woodrow Wilson and Franklin Delano Roosevelt. The final result of his work was a distillation of their philosophies into a single, logical framework for success he called *The 17 Natural Laws of Success*.

One of the greatest discoveries of Hill's work was that every successful person he interviewed had a definite major purpose for their life and they were keenly in tune with that purpose. Each had a plan for fulfilling his or her life purpose and each devoted the greatest part of his or her thoughts and efforts to that goal. Hill would go on to say that, "definiteness of purpose is the starting point of all achievement."

> *"This is the true joy in life, being used for a purpose recognized as a mighty one … the being a force of nature instead of a feverish, selfish little clod of ailments and grievances, complaining that the world will not devote itself to making you happy."*
> George Bernard Shaw

The common tendency is to go through life like a ship with no rudder, no compass, and no map, buffeted to and fro by the waves of life. We tend to go about our daily lives busier than imaginable, but with no real understanding of what we are accomplishing from day to day. It's simply not enough to be busy. Even the ants are busy! We must be busy about doing the RIGHT things … those things for which we were purposed. That brings us to the second Key to Extraordinary Living.

Plan your life and live your passion.

We all have a purpose. That is not the question. The real question is what is your purpose? Author Robert Byrne suggests, "The purpose of life is to live a life of purpose." The Apostle Paul tells us that God is the author of our purpose:

"… for it is God who works in you to will and to act according to his good purpose."

Philippians 2:13

CLARIFYING TERMS

The terms vision, mission, purpose, and goals have been used interchangeably and even misused to the point that there may be some confusion around the use of them here. Perhaps a bit of clarification is in order so that we are all on the same page. To start, purpose and mission have very similar meanings and are often used interchangeably. For this discussion, we will use the word purpose.

Peter Senge in *The Fifth Discipline* helped to put some clarity around the use of these terms. According to Senge, a purpose is an individual's sense of why he or she is alive – it's a calling. It is similar to direction or a general heading. Vision, on the other hand, is a specific destination … a picture of the ultimate or desired future. Purpose tends to be more

The common tendency is to go through life like a ship with no rudder, no compass, and no map, buffeted to and fro by the waves of life.

abstract in nature while vision tends to be more concrete. For instance, prior to JFK, the purpose of the space program was "to improve our ability to explore the heavens." In a speech in May of 1961, JFK crystallized that purpose into a clear vision. He said we'd "have a man on the moon by the end of the 1960s." In 1969, that vision became a reality when Neil Armstrong became the first man to step foot on the surface of the moon.

Purpose also tends to be more permanent while a vision can change with time. For instance, a saw is made for a purpose … to cut. It was not made to hammer, it was not made to stir, nor was it made to measure. It was made to cut. However, the vision for how a particular saw will impact the future can change as time passes. A saw in the hands of our grandfather might be used to cut down the trees that would become his home. That same saw, passed down to our father, might be used to cut firewood for heating. The purpose of the saw did not change. The vision for how that saw would make a difference did.

A purpose tends to be more permanent, while a vision can change with time.

The purpose of the space program remains to be the exploration of the heavens. However, we've fulfilled JFK's vision of landing on the moon and are now exploring Mars and beyond. A true purpose, appropriately defined, remains constant. Our vision for making that purpose come alive, changes to fit our circumstances.

A purpose is what gives our life meaning. It's what drives us to get out of bed in the mornings. It's our calling, our reason for living. It's what we were meant to do. Once we're clear on our purpose, we are able to establish a vision for our lives-where we want to be or what we want our lives to look like in three, five, or even 10 years. It is not important that this vision be a grandiose document that is beautifully crafted and eloquently written. A vision is simply a description of a specific point, some time in the future.

"There may be no heroic connotation to the word persistence, but that quality is to the character of the human being what carbon is to steel."

Napoleon Hill

Clearly we want the vision for our lives to be congruent with our purpose or calling. If it's not, it will be impossible for us to experience fulfillment, no matter how much we achieve. Once we clearly understand our purpose in life, and we have a clear vision for the next few years, we then establish interim goals with specific deadlines or target dates to take us there. If this seems like it is an over-simplification, it's important to know that it is not a difficult process.

PURPOSE FUELS PERSISTENCE

It's commonly recognized that persistence is a trait that underpins the success of people every day. Stories abound of people who have seemingly faced insurmountable obstacles, yet through tenacity and persistence, ultimately achieved great things.

Psychiatrist M. Scott Peck wrote *The Road Less Traveled* – a book that was on the bestseller list for over 12 years. The first three words of this highly acclaimed book are, "Life is difficult." Dr. Peck calls that reality one of the "greatest truths of life." Once we understand and accept that fact, we can live more effectively. He goes on to say that by understanding that life is difficult and usually unfair, instead of merely moaning and groaning about our problems, we can focus on finding ways to solve them.

We all have a purpose. That is not the question. The real question is, "What IS your purpose?

One of the significant differences between successful people and people who fail is the manner in which they approach life's difficulties. Failures tend to wallow in self-pity, or at the very least try to avoid the difficulties of life. This often prevents them from taking the necessary risks required to ultimately find success. Successful people, on the other hand, tackle their problems head-on. They know that life is difficult and they enter each set of circumstances with that knowledge. This perspective helps to enable the persistence required to eventually prevail over any potential obstacle.

One important fact about having a strong guiding purpose is that it fuels persistence. In the face of distraction and obstacles, it is often difficult to continue toward our ultimate destination. However, when we have a definite purpose and a clear vision for the future, that persistence becomes much easier and much more natural.

EXAMPLES OF PERSISTENCE

Thomas Edison is probably the poster-child for persistence. According to legend, his only teacher referred to him as "addled," (i.e. confused or mentally uncertain) and said that he was not worth schooling. However, Edison filed a patent on the average of every two weeks during his entire adult life, holding a total of more than 1,000 patents. One of his most notable accomplishments was the invention of the light bulb. Legend has it that Edison made 10,000 attempts to get the invention to work, failing miserably each time. Describing his lack of success, he said, "I've not

> *"Being busy does not always mean real work. The object of all work is production or accomplishment and to either of these ends there must be forethought, system, planning, intelligence, and honest purpose, as well as perspiration. Seeming to do is not doing.*
> Thomas Edison (1847 – 1931)

failed. I've just found 10,000 ways that won't work." Persistence, fueled by a sense of purpose and a creative vision drove Edison to success.

Florence Nightingale took on the huge challenge of upgrading hospital standards, improving patient care, improving sanitation practices, and promoting nursing education. She almost single-handedly transformed the hospital from a place where people go to die, to a place where people develop hope and healing.

Nightingale faced many obstacles along the way. One of them was her own undefined illness that severely restricted the activity of her adult life. However, she was dedicated to her purpose of caring for injured soldiers and ailing people. She clung to her vision of turning hospitals into places of hope and healing.

Nightingale got up before daylight every day during the Crimean War (1854 – 1856) to head for the battlefields, where British soldiers were dying unnecessarily due to inferior medical care. After the war she returned to her home in England where, although restricted to her sick bed, she managed to establish the Nightingale School and Home for Nurses in London. At age 40, she created and led a medical revolution from her bed and continued to lead those efforts until her death at age ninety. The persistence of Florence Nightingale, fueled by her sense of purpose and her vision for safe, effective health care has eased the pain of countless people over the ages.

Persistence is a unique mental strength required to combat repeated rejection. It's pretending we are a postage stamp … that is we stick to something until we get where we intend to go. Of this we are absolutely certain … persistence receives its fuel from a strong sense of purpose and a clear vision for the future.

FINDING YOUR PURPOSE

We tend to make the task of finding one's life purpose to be a monumental one. It does require a considerable amount of thoughtful reflection, introspection, and prayer. But as discussed before, it is not a difficult task. It's simply a matter of taking inventory of what you're good at doing, what you love to do, and what you feel deep in your heart you should be doing, then summarizing those into some very clear, concise statements that are used to guide your life. One important thing to remember is that your purpose ... your calling ... is something you discover, it's not something you choose. We all have a calling ... a purpose for which we were created. Once we discover that calling, life takes on a whole new meaning.

We experience peace and fulfillment when our daily activities are aligned with our purpose. When we do not act in a manner consistent with our purpose, we experience stress, displeasure, and sometimes even depression. By translating our purpose into a clear concise vision for the future, we dramatically increase the personal fulfillment we experience as we pursue our calling.

In his writings, the Apostle Paul clearly stated that each of us has our own knowledge, natural gifts, abilities, and skills.

"We have different gifts, according to the grace given us. If a man's gift is prophesying, let him use it in proportion to his faith. If it is serving, let him serve; if it is teaching, let him teach; if it is encouraging, let him encourage; if it is contributing to the needs of others, let him give generously; if it is leadership, let him govern diligently; if it is showing mercy, let him do it cheerfully."

Romans 12: 6-8

The secret is to discover your own personal gifts, skills and abilities and identify where they intersect with your passions … your natural dreams, hopes, ambitions, and desires. When you clearly understand this intersection and you take the next step of articulating it in terms of your strengths, your passions, and your purpose, you have planted the seeds of greatness in your life. If you alter your life direction (and your daily activities) to be congruent with these three things, you will achieve more than you ever thought possible. In addition, you'll experience more peace and personal fulfillment along the way.

We experience peace and fulfillment when our daily activities are aligned with our values, beliefs, and passions.

Again, to discover your purpose you simply inventory the things you have a burning desire to do, followed by those things that you are really good at doing. Finally, you should give some thought to the things you feel deep down in your heart that you should be doing. By walking systematically through these steps, you'll begin to see recurring themes that likely will end up as significant components of your life purpose. To make this task easier, we recommend you download a free copy of The Abundance Principle Purpose Finder located under the "downloads" tab at www.AbundantLifeProject.com. Remember, your calling is not something you decide or choose … it's something you discover.

CRAFTING YOUR VISION

Once you have a solid understanding of your purpose, a clear vision for the future will begin to create a road map to your destination over the next few years. As you start this process, it's good to ask a series of questions to ensure you craft the best vision for the future.

- What does your life look like three, five and ten years from now?

- Specifically, what have you achieved in the same length of time?

- How can you pursue your purpose in a manner that impacts the most people for good?

- How can you pursue your purpose in a manner that results in the most personal fulfillment for you and those around you?

Your calling is not something you decide or choose ... it's something you discover.

As you consider these questions, it often helps to think about them in terms of the major categories of your life. The following areas may serve as a primer for thinking in terms of your major life categories:

- **Spiritual Life** – How is your relationship with God? Have much will you have grown spiritually ten years from now? What will your devotional practices look like?

- **Relationships, including Family** – How are your relationships within your family? How do you spend your time with your family? How would your family members describe their relationships with you? What do the relationships in your life look like 10 years from now?

- **Career or Vocation** – What does your career look like in five years? In 10 years? What things will you have accomplished by that time?

- **Finances** – What is the status of your financial condition? How much salary are you earning annually in five years? How about ten years from now? How much money do you have in savings & investments? What is your net worth? How much money are you giving away every year?

- **Lifestyle** – How do you spend your free time? What does your house look like? What does a typical day look like for you?

A PURPOSE REQUIRES A PLAN

Unfortunately having a strong guiding purpose and clear, articulate vision are not enough. Just as we do not arrive at our travel destinations by accident, fulfilling our life calling or achieving our vision doesn't occur by accident either. We must develop a crisp, clear plan for pursuing our purpose so that we can measure our progress on a regular basis.

Plans are often best stated in terms of goals and key actions. Goals are merely interim milestones that help us fulfill our purpose or take us closer to the achievement of a particular vision. We can't boil the ocean all at once, but theoretically, we could boil it one saucepan at a time. Goals and associated key actions help us to "boil the ocean."

> *We can't boil the ocean all at once, but we can boil it one saucepan at a time. Goals and key actions help us to boil the ocean.*

Sometimes a vision can be so overwhelming we become paralyzed by the fear of tackling it. But the important thing to remember is that anything can be done if it's broken down into small chunks. The same truth applies to achieving your vision. The idea is to break it up into manageable goals and the specific activities required to achieve them. For each goal, you should identify 3-5 key actions that you will take on a regular basis to achieve that goal.

Having spent a large part of our professional lives in roles where part of our responsibility was the coaching and development of other people – both students and professionals, we are convinced that the most under-taught subject in homes, schools, colleges, and workplaces today is the subject of achievement planning, goal setting, and progress monitoring. Personal achievement is literally nothing more than a series of small steps toward an expected outcome. If you don't have an expected outcome, personal achievement will elude you. If you don't break the path to that expected outcome down into individual steps, achievement will evade you as well. The type of achievement or success makes no difference.

> *"I never ran 1000 miles.*
> *I could never have done*
> *that. I ran one mile*
> *1000 times."*
> Stu Mittleman
> (Ultra-distance Runner)

Pursuing a clearly defined life purpose and a clear vision for the future is absolutely essential to Extraordinary Living. As the adage taken from a conversation between Alice and the Cheshire Cat in *Alice in Wonderland* says, "If you don't know where you're going, any road will take you there." We must know where we're going, and make specific plans to get there.

We close our discussion of the second Key to Extraordinary Living with a story told in *Christianity Today* by John Huffman. It relates the account of Billy Graham speaking to a group in Charlotte, North Carolina. After many wonderful things were said about him, Graham stepped to the podium and said, "I'm reminded today of Albert Einstein, the great physicist honored by *Time* magazine as the Man of the Century. Einstein was once traveling from Princeton on a train when the conductor came down the aisle, punching the tickets of each passenger. When he came to Einstein, Einstein reached in his vest pocket. He couldn't find his ticket, so he reached in his other pocket.

> *"If you don't know where you're going, you'll end up somewhere else."*
>
> Yogi Berra

It wasn't there. He looked in his briefcase but couldn't find it. He looked in the seat next to him, but couldn't find it. The conductor said, 'Dr. Einstein, I know who you are. We all know who you are. I'm sure you bought a ticket. Don't worry about it.' Einstein nodded appreciatively.

The conductor continued down the aisle punching tickets. As he was ready to move to the next car, he turned around and saw the great physicist on his hands and knees looking under his seat for his ticket. The conductor rushed back. 'Dr. Einstein, don't worry,' he said. "I know who you are. No problem. You don't need a ticket. I'm sure you bought one.' "Einstein said, "Young man, I too know who I am. What I don't know is where I'm going."

That's a great story to illustrate that even one of the smartest men in the world sometimes struggled with staying on task … with keeping his eyes on his intended destination. But the story doesn't stop there. In order to punctuate the point, Dr. Graham continued, "See the suit I'm wearing? I bought it for this luncheon and one more occasion. This is the suit in which I'll

Pursuing a clearly defined life purpose and a creative vision for the future is absolutely essential to Extraordinary Living.

be buried. But when you hear I'm dead, I don't want you to immediately remember the suit I'm wearing. I want you to remember this: I not only know who I am, I also know where I'm going."

Dr. Graham's life purpose beckons him to persist through all things, so that purpose might be realized. And so it is with you. You only have to find out what your real life purpose actually is. And it's never too late. No matter your age, you too can plan your life and live your passion!

THE SECOND KEY TO EXTRAORDINARY LIVING –
"PLAN YOUR LIFE AND LIVE YOUR PASSION"

KEY POINTS

- Every successful person has a definite major life purpose and is keenly in tune with that purpose.

- Many people go through life like a ship with no rudder, no compass, and no map, buffeted to and fro by the waves of life.

- We all have a purpose. The real question is, "What is your purpose?"

- According to Peter Senge, a purpose is our life calling. It's about knowing why we're here. It is similar to direction or a general heading.

- Vision is a specific destination … a picture of the desired future.

- In order for us to experience fulfillment, the vision for our lives need to be congruent with our purpose.

- Persistence is a trait that underpins the success of people every day.

- Because of a persistence that is fueled by a strong sense of their guiding purpose, successful people tackle their problems head-on.

- One important thing to remember is that your purpose … your calling … is not something you choose, it's something you discover.

- When you clearly understand where your natural knowledge, skills, and abilities intersect with your dreams, hopes, and ambitions, and you take the next step of articulating it in terms of your strengths, your passions, and your purpose, you have planted the seeds of greatness in your life.

- Having a clear, articulate purpose is not enough. We must develop a crisp, clear plan for pursuing our purpose.

- Plans are often best stated in terms of goals and key actions. Goals are merely interim milestones that help take us closer to our desired result.

- Pursuing a clearly defined life purpose and a clear vision for the future is absolutely essential to extraordinary living.

KEY ACTIONS

- Visit our website (www.AbundantLifeProject.com) and download your free copy of The Abundance Principle Purpose Finder.

- Spend the time necessary to discover your calling. Pray about it, seek input from trusted friends, search the Scriptures, complete The Purpose Finder … do whatever it takes to get a clear handle on your life purpose.

- Create a vision for your life, and perhaps the life of your family, in all major categories over the next three, five and/or ten years.

- Conduct an inventory of your daily activities and where you spend your time. Are these activities consistent with or in conflict with your life purpose? Are they taking you closer to or further from the vision for your life? Take the necessary steps to ensure that these things are appropriately synchronized.

- Establish 1-2 goals and 3-5 key actions for each major area of your life. Make sure that these goals will move you toward your vision. Review your goals every day and develop a mechanism to track progress against these goals on a regular basis.

CHAPTER FIVE

Living in Relationship

"Love your neighbor as yourself."

Matthew 22:39

"It is hard to imagine a more pitiful existence than life on the streets of Calcutta, or in one of its slums, or making a living there as a prostitute. Yet despite the poverty and squalor they face, people with these lives are much happier than you might imagine." That was the surprising discovery made by authors Robert Holmes, Kurt Kleiner, Kate Douglas, and Michael Bond, which they wrote about in a *Readers Digest* article entitled, "10 Keys to True Happiness." The article cited data gathered from the slums of Calcutta and concluded that friendship, one of the ten keys, plays a major role in people's lives regardless of social status.

In the study, people were interviewed from each of the three social groups previously mentioned. The "Life Satisfaction" levels in all three groups, while well below those in more favored environments, were not too far off the mark of a control group which consisted of middle class students from the city. The authors summarized the study by saying, "We think social relationships are partly responsible." They pointed out that each of the three groups received high marks in specific areas like family and friends. "Slum dwellers did particularly well, perhaps because they are most likely to be able to cash in on the social support that arises from the importance of the extended family in Indian culture," according to the authors.

Friendship plays a major role in people's lives, regardless of social status.

The reality is we do need each other. In fact, we are at our best when we are interacting with other people. When you think about it, mankind was created to live in fellowship. First was fellowship with God, then fellowship with each other. If you remember the story of creation in Genesis, God noticed, after he had created Adam that, "it was not good for man to be alone." The result was that from the rib of Adam, God formed a woman. Eve was created to have fellowship with Adam.

And so it is with all of us. Jesus himself made an interesting statement when He said one day that the two greatest commandments any of us could keep were to love God, and love others. Relationships! This brings us to the third Key to Extraordinary Living:

Build and maintain strong relationships.

All of us have something inside us which we can invest in someone else. Conversely, we should be willing to receive what others wish to invest in us. It is the nature of why we were created. The simple truth is that none of us was placed on this earth to live in isolation.

Perhaps you are familiar with the majestic sequoia trees of California. It's a bit surprising to learn that these massive trees have a very shallow root system. Their ability to stand is insured by the fact that the roots of all the trees are intertwined. Each tree lends support to the others to stand strong. The same is true for people. We are at our best when we are supported by, and stand in support of, others.

Author and speaker Mark Victor Hansen is fond of saying, "When you hold up one finger all you have is one. Hold up two fingers and all of a sudden you have 11." There is a synergy that exists when two or more people combine in a relationship. We all need each other. While there are a few people out there who enjoy being alone all the time, most of us need others to bring light to our lives.

SOLITARY CONFINEMENT

One of the startling facts about today's society is that people have become increasingly solitary through self-seclusion. There was a day when people wandered the neighborhood and everyone knew his neighbor. A second thought was never given to sending your child next door to borrow a cup of milk.

None of us was placed on earth to live in isolation. We were created to live in relationship with others.

Today, however, we have closed ourselves in and we barely know the people around us. The tragedy is, this is not only a phenomenon in our neighborhoods and work places. It exists within the four walls of our homes. Today, children are self-contained in their rooms. With stereos, computers, telephones, the Internet, and so much more, the only time some children come out of their rooms is to eat.

We've all heard the stories of school shootings and postal office massacres. Many times the family living under the same roof with the perpetrator had no inclination that something was amiss. Unless we all develop our ability to relate to one another, beginning in the family room, we are destined to become more and more isolated.

> *One of the greatest things we can do in life is to love our neighbor.*

Jesus said that one of the greatest things we can do in life is to love our neighbor. Right? But if you are familiar with the story, you also know that he said more. He didn't just say to love our neighbor, he actually said, "Love your neighbor as yourself."

Some people have trouble with the "yourself" part. Perhaps one of the reasons we sometimes have trouble feeling good about others is because we do not feel good about ourselves. Let's reverse that concept. If you and I are not relating well with (loving) ourselves, we may not be able to really love someone else. If we are not taking care of ourselves, it may be hard for us to care for our neighbor. If we are having trouble with our past, it definitely affects our present and likely even our future.

This is where some advice from Chapter Three is useful. We must get over it! We must put our past behind us and move on. Sometimes that means seeking professional counseling. Sometimes it means praying for emotional healing. Remember, Extraordinary Living is about being a victor, not a victim.

BUILDING WALLS INSTEAD OF RELATIONSHIPS

For most of us, it is much easier to build walls than it is to build relationships. It's not uncommon, especially in the workplace to have one or more "strained" relationships. We may have a negative or otherwise antagonistic encounter with someone that starts the "wall-building" process and we build it higher and higher every time we engage with each other from that point forward.

Sir Winston Churchill and Lady Astor provide a classic example of "wall-building." These two prominent British politicians are responsible for one of the more bitter relationships in history. The interactions between them were constantly filled with sarcasm, conflict, and caustic remarks – each intending to "one-up" the other.

One particular day during a debate between the two in Parliament, Lady Astor shouted to Churchill, "Sir Winston, if you were my husband, I'd poison your tea." Churchill quickly retorted, "Lady Astor, if you were my wife, I'd drink it!"

On another occasion after Churchill had consumed a large amount of alcohol, Lady Astor sensed he was inebriated and snapped, "Mr. Prime Minister, I perceive that you are drunk." Churchill replied with a slight smile, "You are correct, Lady Astor, and I perceive that you are ugly. But tomorrow, I shall be sober."

Sometimes it's easier to build walls than it is to build relationships

When we get cross-ways with a colleague, a friend, or a family member, it is so easy for us to build walls between us and then use every interaction as a means to reinforce that separation. Rather than taking the initial step to remove just one brick from the wall, we resort to building the wall taller and thicker every time our paths cross.

One of the reasons meaningful relationships do not abound is because people don't know how to build relationships. We might surround ourselves with people, but that does not mean we will be successful in forming and growing our relationships. Before we can build strong relationships, we must learn how to be a friend. In fact, the best way to get and keep a friend is to be a friend ourselves. Here are some tips to get us started:

- **Be an Encourager**

A worthy goal for us all is to make a point to encourage someone every day. There are hundreds of ways this can be done. We can compliment the way they look (tastefully), acknowledge their work efforts, or compliment them on their family. We all love to hear something good about ourselves. The sad truth is that most people just assume no one really notices or cares. The first building block in constructing meaningful relationships is simply to build others up.

Once again the Apostle Paul gives great advice for being an encourager:

"Do not let any unwholesome talk come out of your mouths, but only what is helpful for building others up according to their needs, that it may benefit those who listen."

Ephesians 4:29

- **Be a Quick Forgiver**

Here is a truth. Some of the people with whom you need to be in relationship right now, and are not, are supposed to be the very closest to you on earth. However, something has happened, words were exchanged, actions were taken, perhaps a trust was violated. As a

92

result, lifelong friendships came to an end. Maybe you are a Churchill and your Lady Astor is a spouse, a sibling, a parent, or a child. Maybe your Lady Astor is a former friend.

The reality is, people are going to hurt you. And chances are good, that those who will hurt you most will likely come from your inner circle – someone who is close to you – who knows you better than most. Perhaps you confided in them. Maybe you made yourself vulnerable to them. You probably *The reality is, people are going to hurt us. Those that hurt us most tend to come from our inner circle.* trusted them. And then one day, when you least expected it, they launched an attack that you cannot now, nor ever will understand.

Right now you need to make an intentional decision. Either you will rise above the circumstances and forgive them, or you will get lost in the muck and mire of self-pity, resentment, and bitterness. The worst thing you can do is to continue harboring resentment. If you do, you will be tempted to never again get close to another person, nor let anyone else get close to you. The best way to keep relationships alive is to decide ahead of time that you will always be a quick forgiver no matter what.

• Be a Good Listener

Some have said that God gave us two ears and one mouth for a reason. That reason is due to our tendency to try and impress the world with our great wisdom. We all have something to say – unfortunately, some more than others. One of the best things you can do for another person is to give them the gift of your ears. I (Tim) can't tell you the number of times I have "counseled" people and never said a word. I just let them talk, talk, talk and talk some more. In the end

93

they have given me a hug and said, "Thank you so much. You don't know how much you have helped me today." I had done nothing but listen and they thought I was the greatest counselor in the world.

When it comes to being a friend, be a good listener. It is actually a sign of wisdom. Solomon, the wisest man in the world once wrote: "Do not be quick with your mouth … let your words be few." (Ecclesiastes 5:2).

A speaker once told the following story about becoming a better listener. While at a speaking engagement where he was to be the keynote speaker, the host met him at the door and began to describe the events of the night. The speaker's mind was occupied with his responsibilities for the evening and was not tuned in to what the host was saying. He responded occasionally with the gratuitous "uh huh" to give the impression he was really listening. The host eventually walked away, at which time the speaker's wife poked him in the arm. "What's the matter with you?" she inquired. The speaker was shocked by her question and uncharacteristic intensity. "Do you have any idea what that man just said to you?" She asked. "Sure," replied her husband. "He was just giving me the normal run down and time line." "No!" she quickly retorted. "He just told you that his mother passed away last night. And all you said was 'uh huh!'" If we are to build strong relationships with others, we must give them our attention and we must learn to listen.

> "In your anger do not sin. Do not let the sun go down while you are still angry."
> Ephesians 4:26

Who has been trying to get your attention lately? Your spouse? Your kids? Your employees? Your boss? God? Think about it, really. Do you spend most of your days with your mouth open and your ears closed? Are you more inclined to tell people what you're thinking rather then listen to what they're saying? Are your conversations consumed with making you the center of attention? When the attention shifts from you to another person do you try to gain it back? And if you cannot, do you move on to another person or group? God gave us two ears and one mouth … we should be careful to use them in the proper proportion.

- **Be a Laugher**

Lighten up already. Don't take life so seriously. Every circumstance of life isn't life-altering and doesn't have to be serious. Take time – no, make time to lighten up and have some fun. The reality is that, even as adults, we have an enormous capacity to do really stupid things. Give yourself a break. Learn to laugh it off and you'll be better for it.

Have you ever noticed that the people who are always laughing and cutting up seem to have the most people surrounding them? That's because we love to be around people who laugh and have fun. We are drawn to them. We have an innate desire to exercise our funny bone. Learn to laugh more. It's good for you. Solomon once wrote, "A cheerful heart is good medicine." (Proverbs 17:22).

We have an enormous capacity to do really stupid things.

People who take life too seriously don't usually enjoy life all that much. In fact, the stress of anxious living and a joyless existence can actually shorten one's life. If you find yourself bankrupt in the area of meaningful relationships, you might consider whether you are standing in the rain or the sunshine in the parade of life.

- **Be someone who says, "I love you."**

"I love you." What a powerful phrase. Go ahead. Say it aloud three or four times. It seems so easy to say – just three simple words. You would think this popular phrase would fall quickly and easily from the lips of most anyone ... but not so. Take myself (Tim) for instance. For some reason the words "I love you" were difficult for me to utter as an adult. I can honestly say that what brought a change into my life in this area was the woman I married.

When Jamie became my wife, I married into the most love-expressing family I had ever known. I still remember the first time I went with her to a family reunion. I thought I would be "I love you'd" to death. These were people who didn't even know me. For me it was way off the charts. I wanted to find a place to hide. The problem was the only place I could find was an outhouse in the State Park where we were meeting. Nearly 22 years have come and gone since I married Jamie. I can safely say that she has broken me of my "I love you" blockage. She has taught me how to express my feelings. Now it comes fairly easily. Not a day goes by without me telling Jamie, "I love you." The same goes for my parents.

I also take great joy as a father in regularly expressing my love to my teenage kids. "I love you's" are exchanged regularly before departures to school, Friday night activities, church trips, and before bed each night. Occasionally, our kids will call out from their beds, "I love you!" If we do not respond quickly enough to suit them, they will repeat the line with growing intensity until someone responds. It is all just part of the way we live.

Why is it that we have trouble expressing our love for others? Could it be that in doing so we make ourselves vulnerable? We set ourselves up to be hurt. What if our expression of love is rejected?

Then what would we do? That type of fear should never exist within family relationships; however, in many homes it does exist and it is very real. The dysfunction among family members might be so great that expressing any emotion can be dangerous. In such cases, that part of our natural makeup can get locked down, suppressed, maybe even forgotten. In those instances, knowing how to express love, and express it authentically, is never learned. The good news is that anyone can begin loving others, regardless of the emotional baggage existing in their lives.

Society has taught us that love is about feeling. We have been taught that we "fall in love" with our spouses and so conversely it's been made Okay to "fall out of love" with them, too. The focus is on the feeling. Scripture tells us that true love is about giving and doing. Love is an action first and it's a feeling second. The Apostle Paul wrote:

"Love is patient, love is kind. It does not envy, it does not boast, it is not proud. It is not rude, it is not self-seeking, it is not easily angered, it keeps no record of wrongs. Love does not delight in evil but rejoices with the truth. It always protects, always trusts, always hopes, always perseveres. Love never fails."

1 Corinthians 13: 4-8

Years ago, Jackie Deshannon popularized the song, *"What the World Needs Now is Love Sweet Love."* That fact is still true today, but to our own detriment, many of us do not realize it.

One of the sweetest blessings of life is to be loved and to have someone to love in return. However, one of the greatest challenges we face is being the one to make the first move. Someone in your life needs to be told they are loved by you – probably more than one. If you are a natural at this, then you will not need the words that follow. But if you are in pursuit of Extraordinary Living, you cannot overlook this assignment. It may be risky. It may even set you up for disappointment and even rejection. But remember, love is more about giving then receiving.

Love must be a verb before it can become a noun.

Make a list of people that you really care about. Ask yourself, "Have I ever told this person I love them?" It may be your parent(s), your grandparent(s), perhaps it's your sibling(s), your spouse, or your children. It may by a close friend. It may even be the one with whom you hope to spend the rest of your life. Tell them you love them. Go ahead – you'll be glad you did.

TAKING RISKS

To build strong relationships we must be willing to take risks and to endure hardships on behalf of those relationships. The greatest relationship in the world is the one God established with us – His creation. Through the sacrificial acts of Jesus, God risked everything to express his unquestionable love for us. Furthermore, Jesus gave up everything – to live and die just like us – so that we might learn how to live and die. The Scriptures declare:

> *"Greater love has no one than this, that he lay down his life for his friends."*
>
> John 15:13

That's sometimes hard for us to conceive. Can we really have a relationship with another person so strong that it would cause us to lay down our life on their behalf? Is that even possible?

The question itself reminds us of a story about a family who had two boys, one of whom became gravely ill. The parents were told that unless the boy had a blood transfusion, he would surely die in a matter of days. Therefore, a search ensued for the proper blood type. Naturally, family members were the first to be tested and it was found that the sick boy's younger brother had the matching blood type. The parents explained the situation to the younger boy, who quickly agreed to the procedure that would save his older brother's life. On the day of the blood transfusion the small tyke was especially nervous, yet still completely willing to follow through. As his little arms were punctured and the life-giving blood was collected, tears began to well up in the boys eyes. His mother asked if he was in pain. "No," he squeaked. "But do you know how long it will be before I die?" Suddenly the horrified mother realized that all along, the younger brother thought that to save his brother's life meant he would have to lose his. Soon tears were dried and relief settled into the room as his mother explained that just a couple of pints were needed and that all would be well. In the end the little brother's sacrifice did save his big brother's life.

Is there someone in your life for whom you would be willing to pay the ultimate sacrifice? Do you have strong relationships for which you would be willing to endure true hardship? Having those kinds of relationships open us up to a whole new type of living.

At the end of the day, we all need relationships in order to be most fulfilled. We were not created to live in solitary confinement. We were created to live in relationship. Whether you have existing relationships that need mending, or you have potential relationships that need to be planted and cultivated, start the process today. If you are to experience extraordinary living, you must build and maintain strong relationships. Go for it!

THE THIRD KEY TO EXTRAORDINARY LIVING –
"BUILD AND MAINTAIN STRONG RELATIONSHIPS"

KEY POINTS

- Mankind was created for the purpose of fellowship. First with God, then with each other.

- Jesus said the two greatest commandments were to love God and love others.

- A startling fact about today's society is that people have become increasingly solitary through self-seclusion.

- In order to feel good about others, we need to arrive at a place where we feel good about ourselves.

- We must learn to put our past behind us and move on. We must get over it!

- It's much easier for many of us to build walls than it is to build relationships.

- Relationships are formed by encouraging, listening, forgiving, laughing, and saying "I love you."

- We love to be around people who laugh and have fun. We're drawn to them. Learn to laugh more. It's good for you.

- Society has taught us that love is about feeling. Scripture tells us that true love is about doing. It's an action first, and then it's a feeling.

- To build strong relationships we must be willing to take risks and to endure hardship on behalf of those relationships.

- God, through the sacrificial acts of Jesus Christ, gave up everything for us … so that we might live in relationship with Him.

KEY ACTIONS

- Make a complete list of those you really consider your close friends. Ask yourself some questions about the nature of the relationships. Are they strong or weak? Does complete trust exist in both directions? Are there issues that need to be resolved? How can you improve the relationship? Ask for forgiveness where you know you should.

- Make a list of people who have hurt you and/or for whom you may have some feelings of animosity, anger, or resentment. Forgive them, regardless of what they've done or the pain they may have caused. Once you forgive them, consider "clearing the air" between you. At the very least, make a point to free yourself of the burden of resentment.

- For the next 30 days, commit to positively and verbally encouraging at least five persons each day. Start with those closest to you, but also include those with whom you are only acquainted, as well as a few strangers. Performing random acts of kindness is a great way to plant the seeds of great relationships.

- In discussions with others, make a mental note of your listening habits. Are you thinking about what to say next, or are you really listening to the other person? Ask one or two people to give you feedback on your listening skills, habits, and tendencies.

- Make a list of people to whom you need to say "I Love You" and then do it!

CHAPTER SIX

Master or Servant

"The difference between poor people and rich people is easy. The poor spend their money and then save what's left over; the rich save their money and then spend what's left over."

Jim Rohn, Author & Speaker

An immigrant from Hungary is said to have migrated to the United States and opened a street-side vegetable stand. The quality of his produce coupled with his great prices soon required him to expand. After a period of time, his small street-side produce stand grew into a chain of 10-12 grocery stores.

Upon graduating college and receiving his CPA, the man's youngest son returned to work in the family business. He was appalled by his father's lack of financial sophistication and his rudimentary accounting system. On one side of the cash register was a small cigar box which contained all of the accounts-payable invoices. Cash from his daily sales were placed in the cash register and receipts for paid bills were placed in a cigar box on the other side of the register.

"Father," the boy remarked, "it is impossible to run your business successfully with this crude system. How do you know what your profits are?" "Well son," the father replied, "when I came to this country I had nothing but the shirt on my back. I started my business from scratch and today your brother is an engineer. Your sister is a doctor, and you are a CPA. We have a nice house, a decent car, and a vacation home on the lake. Our business is booming and everything we own is completely paid for ... Now, add all of those things together, subtract the shirt, and that is our profit."

BACK TO THE BASICS

Personal financial management is not a difficult process, but it does require a plan and the discipline to follow that plan. Unfortunately, consumer debt and the promise of a higher standard of living often lure us away from the basic financial planning required to live an abundant life.

The great football coach Vince Lombardi would, on occasion hold up a football before his players and say, "Gentlemen, this is a football." Coach Lombardi knew the importance of reviewing the basics on a regular basis and he regularly taught his players the fundamentals required for success in football.

The basic fundamentals of football are often referred to as blocking and tackling. Using that metaphor in the financial arena, the "blocking and tackling" of money revolves around earning, spending, saving, borrowing, and investing.

If we wish to live extraordinary lives we must recognize that debt is a tool to be used intelligently. We must learn that an extraordinary life is a financially disciplined life ... one in which conscious decision-making occurs with even the most trivial spending. We must fully comprehend that borrowing to purchase expendable items or rapidly depreciating assets using credit cards or bank loans is flirting with a trip to the poorhouse.

That brings us to the fourth Key to Extraordinary Living:

No matter how much you earn, spend less.

We recognize that the manner in which this key is stated may lead you to believe that mastering your money is only about the way you manage your spending habits. That is not true. In fact, you'll notice that the key itself speaks very directly to at least two components of money management – earning and spending money. In addition, this Key speaks more indirectly to the other component of money mastery – what you do with the money you do not spend.

EARNING MONEY

Earning or having a lot of money is neither a sin, nor is it necessarily counter to God's intention for our lives. Unfortunately, many well-meaning people cultivate an expectation that scarcity and sacrifice are required if we are to be Godly people. However, the Bible has numerous stories of Godly people having tremendous wealth.

A couple of examples are Solomon and Job. The wealthiest man who ever lived was King Solomon and when Job proved himself faithful and devoted to God, he was given back twice the wealth and possessions he had lost.

Perhaps you've heard the story of the Good Samaritan. In the story, the Samaritan didn't simply help the injured traveler up and send him on his way. He took care of

> "Make all you can, save all you can, give all you can.
> John Wesley, Founder of Methodism

him both medically and financially. He paid for lodging and he paid for all of the costs associated with his medical care. He was able to do this because he had the financial means to do so. The Good Samaritan had obviously learned how to master his money. When Jesus described the actions of this man, He told us to "Go and do likewise."

A review of the scriptures yields more than 1,000 passages directly related to money and its use. One of the most notable passages is from Paul's letters to Timothy:

> *"The love of money is a root of all kinds of evil. Some people, eager for money, have wandered from the faith and pierced themselves with many griefs."*
>
> 1 Timothy 6: 10

Many people often misunderstand this verse and use it to imply that those who have money are evil or have at least "wandered from the faith." A regularly misquoted translation of this passage is "money is the root of all evil." That is simply wrong on at least two counts. First, "the love of money" is the subject of this sentence, not money – a big difference. Secondly, the love of money is characterized as "a" root of all kinds of evil, as opposed to "the" root. There are those well-meaning Christians who take great pride in holding up their sacrifice and poverty as in keeping with the words of Jesus in this passage.

However, this is clearly a twisting of Jesus' intent behind these words.

Another often misquoted passage comes from Luke 16. In this chapter, Jesus tells the story of a manager who was accused of wasting the possessions of the rich man he served. The man is relieved of his duties and Jesus admonishes us that being trustworthy with little is a precursor to being trusted with much. He goes on to say that if we are not trustworthy in handling someone else's property, who would give us property of our own? He then makes this, sometimes startling statement:

"No servant can serve two masters. Either he will hate the one and love the other, or he will be devoted to the one and despise the other. You cannot serve both God and Money."

Luke 16:13

Again, this passage is often a favorite of those who advocate on behalf of scarcity and sacrifice. Many times it is used to label money as "bad," "evil," and even "ungodly." The problem, however, is not the mere presence of money. The real problem surfaces when we try to serve money, rather than master it. It escalates when we make possessions or earthly treasures our god … when we chase after wealth at the expense of everything else. The key point here is that it is the condition of our hearts, not the condition of our bank accounts that matter.

> *"Money makes a good servant, but a bad master."*
> French Proverb

Often we may chase after money because we are subconsciously feeding the scarcity thinking in our lives. We compare ourselves to others and make judgments about whether we are "measuring up" financially. In Matthew's version of the same story, Jesus speaks of storing up treasures in Heaven as opposed to constantly running after earthly treasures. He goes on to say:

"For where your treasure is, there your heart will be also."

Matthew 6: 21

Jesus is saying that your heart follows your treasures. In other words, your heart follows after that which is of extreme importance to you. If your ultimate goal (your treasure) is to amass earthly possessions merely for the sake of having more, your heart will soon follow. In that pursuit, you'll miss out on the richness of God's guiding presence in your life.

It's the condition of our heart, not the condition of our bank account that matters.

Make no mistake about it. The presence of money can and does enable some people to do very bad things. On the flip side, worlds of good can also be done with money. It takes money to solve the problem of world hunger. It takes money to stamp out AIDS, cancer, heart disease, and other life-threatening illnesses. It takes money to provide for a family whose home has just been destroyed by fire. It takes money to print Bibles and build churches. But conversely, a world of good can also be done by lending a listening ear, by providing a helping hand, or by speaking words that heal. Again, it's the condition of our heart, not the condition of our bank account that matters. We must learn to master our money rather than becoming mastered by it.

SPENDING OUR WAY INTO THE POORHOUSE

In their book titled *The Millionaire Next Door,* Thomas Stanley and William Danko paint a portrait of the average American millionaire with some startling findings from their research. Among the most notable of their findings include:

- The median total annual income of the average millionaire is $131,000. This means that they become millionaires, not usually by earning large sums of money, but by intelligently managing the money they do earn.

- They live well below their means because they value financial security and independence over high social status. On average, their total annual income is less than 7 percent of their total net worth.

- Approximately 80 percent are first-generation affluent, meaning they did not receive an inheritance to jump-start their net worth.

- Approximately 97 percent are homeowners, about half of which have occupied the same homes for more than twenty years.

- On average, they invest about 20 percent of their income while a large majority invest 15 percent each year.

- They are not workaholics. A significant majority work an average of 45 to 55 hours each week.

- They teach their children to be economically self-sufficient as adults.

We don't share these findings to encourage readers to immediately start chasing after millionaire status. We share these findings to help you understand that managing your money intelligently over a period of years can lead to astounding results.

Unfortunately, the urge to spend money today is at an all-time high. We are constantly bombarded by outside pressures from print ads in newspapers and magazines to broadcast ads from our radios, televisions, and computer screens to buy more and more things. In fact, you may have heard the phrase, "We can't save any money because all of our friends keep buying things we don't need." That quip may seem humorous on the surface, but it rings so true for many people and its effects can be devastating.

If we were truthful with ourselves, we would admit that we are a "monthly payment" society. In fact, the first question we ask when shopping for a new car, a new home, or new home furnishings is often, "How much is the payment?" Instead of buying large ticket items on the basis of their value, we buy them on the basis of what we can "afford" each month. This fosters a "cash flow" mentality as opposed to developing a "net worth" approach to personal financial management. As a result, most people live paycheck to paycheck, often one or two checks away from financial ruin.

> *"Any government, like any family can for a year spend a little more than it earns. But you and I know that a continuance of that habit means the poorhouse."*
>
> Franklin D. Roosevelt

Financial Author Ethan Pope describes the two types of people in the world: the savers and the spenders. Pope suggests that the philosophy of the saver is usually: "Get all you can, can all you get, and sit on your can." The philosophy of the spender usually tends to be: "Buy things you don't need, with money you don't have, to impress people you don't even like!" According to Pope, because opposites attract, the odds are better than average that these two types of people will end up marrying each other.

If we're going to live extraordinary lives, we must learn to get a handle on our spending. Two very simple practices can easily and automatically aid in controlling expenses. The first is an exercise everyone should conduct regardless of their current financial conditions. For the next 30 days, track every penny you spend. Take ten to fifteen seconds after each and every purchase and record that purchase by either asking for a receipt, or by recording it on a small note pad. Regardless of the method you choose, record all your expenses and identify the reason for the expenditure (i.e. food, auto fuel, clothing, etc.) You may develop your own set of categories or manner of organizing these expenses, but we recommend something close to the following:

- Food & Groceries

- Clothing

- Dining & Entertainment

- Household Items (Cleaners, Toiletries, Minor Repairs, etc.)

- Automobile

- Insurance

- Utilities

- Consumer Debt (Credit Cards, Bank Loans, etc.)

- Mortgage

- Miscellaneous

By following through on this exercise, you will begin to develop an awareness of your current spending habits. An optional step to expand this process and to make it much easier is to use a basic money management software package to maintain your checkbook and to record all expenses. These packages usually have a "Cash Flow" function that allows you to look at the flow of money in and the flow of money out on a regular basis (Weekly, Monthly, Quarterly, Annually, etc.). We recommend a monthly review of the cash flow report with everyone who makes purchasing decisions in your household, making absolutely certain that actions are taken to bring excessive spending in certain categories under control.

It's hard to save money when all your friends keep buying things you don't need.

In 1991, I (Jeff) bought a computer and a money management software package and began tracking our household expenditures. Lori and I were newlyweds, planning to start a family and wanted to ensure we were managing our money appropriately in order to support our soon-to-be-developing household. You'll remember that back in 1991, the home computer was more expensive than it is today. I think we paid about $2,000 for the computer and printer, using a 12 month interest-free loan from the retailer.

We began to track all of our expenses religiously. Every purchase was subject to being recorded. While we found the immediate change in process a bit tough, it became much easier when we began to "find" money at the end of each month. The amount of money we found was actually surprising. By merely tracking our spending, we found that our spending habits changed almost immediately. Just placing a modest amount of scrutiny on even the most trivial expenditures, knowing that this purchase would be summarized in a "cash flow" report at the end of the month, caused us not to spend so impulsively.

In less than a year we had found enough money to pay for the computer ($2,000). Within 14 months we had paid off the balances of all of our credit card debt. By the 18 month mark, we had retired the debt on one automobile. We'll talk more about debt retirement later on. The point here is that merely by watching and tracking our spending, we altered our spending habits for the good. That little exercise of tracking our spending habits closely changed our lives for the better.

Shortly after retiring the debt on our credit cards and one automobile, Lori began experiencing problems with her first pregnancy. Ultimately, she was required to stop working for approximately seven months, including the maternity leave. This effectively cut our working income in half; however, by changing our spending habits during the preceding year and a half we were able to avert a financial disaster.

The second method to control spending is to invoke a "cooling off period" prior to making impulse purchases of $100 or more. The cooling off period in the Standridge household is a minimum of 24 hours. If we find something that we impulsively wish to purchase and it costs more than $100, we'll invoke the 24 Hour Rule in order to determine if it's really something we want or need. If the desire to purchase is as strong after the full-day wait, then we'll consider purchasing it. It's not a foregone conclusion we'll buy it at that point, but we will more deeply consider the merits of doing so.

By merely tracking your spending, you'll find that your spending habits will change almost immediately

The amount is not as critical as the process. Depending on your level of income, $100 may be way too much. You might want to reduce it to $50 or even $25. That's okay. However, we would suggest you NOT increase that amount beyond $100. That figure is a good "psychological" marker regardless of your income level. This concept of the "cooling off period" has kept us from making a number of rather frivolous purchases in the past.

FIRST THINGS FIRST

A third, more invasive strategy for effectively managing your spending is to establish six major categories of expenditures and to allocate money to these categories each pay-day. This is best executed by establishing separate bank accounts and moving the money automatically before it ever reaches your hands. However, with the right level of tenacity and discipline, it may also be carried out using a cash & envelope system. While most people only give and save from what's left over after everything else has been paid, this strategy advocates paying God and yourself first. The idea is to proactively manage a "spending plan" each month in order to exercise more discipline and financial control.

There are a number of categories that can be used to effectively manage spending; however, the following categories and allocations are recommended:

- 10% - Giving Account (Used for paying tithes and other charitable giving.)

- 10% - Net Worth Account (Used to eliminate consumer debt first and then purchase securities and other passive income-producing assets such as stocks, mutual funds, real estate, etc.)

- 10% - Short-term Savings Account (This is the savings account for emergencies. It should contain a minimum of 3-6 months worth of expenses to rely on during unplanned drops in income.)

- 10% - Education Account (For your personal education as well as the education of your children, if you have or plan to have children).

- 10% - Entertainment Account (Used for recreation, vacations, and etc.)

- 50% - Necessities Account (This is for all required living expenses.)

It may be difficult or even impossible to begin with these specific allocation percentages, but this should be the desired state. In order to effectively execute this strategy, each category should be established and a regular amount of money must be placed in the account every pay-day, regardless of the amount. Rather than immediately starting at the ideal state, it may be that the different amounts look more like this:

- 10% - Giving Account

- 7% - Net Worth Account

- 5% - Short-term Savings Account

- 3% - Education Account

- 5% - Entertainment Account

- 70% - Necessities Account

That's perfectly okay. Establishing the process and diligently placing funds in each account systematically every single pay-day is most important – much more important, quite frankly, than the actual proportion allocated to each account. Slowly, as expenses are reduced relative to income, adjustments can be made to your distribution of funds in order to move toward the desired allocations. The important thing is to start the process and to develop a discipline of funding these accounts automatically, every single month.

DESPERATELY IN DEBT

One of the problems with spending excessively is that our working income seldom provides enough cash to purchase outright some of the do-dads we want. As a result, we choose to incur debt, using credit cards, lines of credit, and bank loans to purchase these things. We think in terms of the monthly payment rather than thinking in terms of "value" or "total cost." As a result, the entire American economy is deeply rooted in and driven by consumer debt. In addition, individuals and families across the country are burdened so much financially, they can hardly see anything but a life of despair.

The important thing is to develop a discipline around your giving, saving & spending.

Not long ago a news release reported that consumer debt is rising twice as rapidly as salaries and that the average household spends 20 percent of its disposable household income on debt payments. Many people regularly deposit money into bank savings accounts paying 1.5% annual interest, while at the same time paying 10% - 20% in credit card interest.

Let us be very clear about one thing. Regular and systematic saving is very important! However, once you have accumulated a "safety net" of liquid cash (usually about 3-6 months worth of expenses), you should begin funneling any extra money into investment vehicles that will allow you to build wealth more quickly. Sometimes those investment vehicles include investing in programs that help you reduce your consumer debt more rapidly. Financial author Dave Ramsey suggests that the best way to reduce your credit card debt is to perform plastic surgery – that is taking out a pair of scissors and cutting up the plastic culprits (credit cards) that get us in trouble in the first place.

Interest from consumer debt is probably the single greatest obstacle to achieving any lasting wealth.

For most people, consumer debt and associated interest is probably the single greatest obstacle to the achievement of any lasting wealth. It very quietly saps us of the money we could be placing into high-yielding investments. Reducing or eliminating this debt however, is nothing more than a numbers game. As we begin diverting idle or discretionary dollars toward the reduction of our debts, we take an enormous step in regaining control of our financial lives.

There are a number of methods, techniques, and software programs designed to accelerate the reduction of outstanding consumer debt. While many of these programs can make the process much easier and perhaps even automated, the following manual steps will also get you started on the right track:

- Identify a set amount of money that you will commit to allocating toward the reduction or elimination of debt every single month. Ideally, this amount will be equivalent to 10% – 20% of your household income. However, if it's only $50 -

$100 per month, that's okay. Do it anyway. We'll call this monthly amount the "Pay-off Accelerator" (PA).

- Rank your debts in order of the most expensive debt to the least expensive debt and number them 1 thru x. Most likely, the order of your list will have credit cards and automobile loans at or near the top due to their normally high interest rates. Usually, home mortgages will appear near the bottom of your list. You might also consider ranking low-balance debt near the top, since it could be paid off quickly.

- Add your PA to your regular monthly payment for Debt #1 from your ranked listing each month until that debt has been completely eliminated.

- When Debt #1 has been completely retired, add the monthly payment from that debt to your PA. Now, apply your newly increased PA to Debt #2 each and every month until that debt has been completely eliminated.

- Continue that process until you have eliminated your consumer debt completely (credit cards, bank loans, home-equity loans, signature loans, etc.)

- Once your consumer debt has been completely eliminated, you should determine if it makes sense to pay down your home mortgage or to place your excess cash into a safe, but high-yielding investment vehicle.

The basic rule of thumb is if the interest rate on your home loan is greater than the annual rate of return you would likely earn from your planned investments, then you should consider paying off your home mortgage also. However, it would be entirely reasonable at this point to split your freed-up cash each month, placing half of it in your high-yielding investment and using the other half to pay down mortgage interest. In all instances, you should consult your financial or investment advisor.

Using a payoff accelerator coupled with rolling your monthly payments together after each debt is retired creates a "snowballing" effect, thus reducing subsequent debts very quickly. It is not uncommon to have several thousand dollars available for investing each month after all debt has been retired.

COMPOUNDING YOUR WEALTH

There is one concept about wealth-building that even the most novice of investor should know. That concept has commonly been referred to as "the magic of compound interest." Albert Einstein, one of the greatest minds of the 20th century called compounding interest, "the greatest mathematical discovery of all times." Perhaps you've heard of the concept before, but let us explain for the sake of clarity.

Simple interest is just that … simple. If you were to take $10,000 and invest it at 5% in a simple interest-bearing vehicle, at the end of one year, you would earn $500. At the end of year two you would earn another $500, year three the same, and so on. Each year the interest is calculated based on the original principal balance of $10,000.

Albert Einstein called compounding interest, "the greatest mathematical discovery of all times."

Compounded interest, on the other hand, is added to the original $10,000 principle so at the end of year one you have $10,500. At the end of year two you would earn interest on the new principal amount, earning approximately $537, year three $564, and so on. Each year the interest is earned on a slightly higher principal amount, thus allowing the money to grow or "compound" over time.

To further illustrate the point, let's assume that two children (Billy and Sally) are born on the same day. Billy's parents decide to start a college fund, and make a $5,000 initial deposit in an investment that yields 5% annually. They also agree to deposit $25.00 in the account on a monthly basis. When Billy is ready to begin college, his fund will only have amassed $22,386.72.

Sally's parents decide to do something similar. They start a college fund for her in an investment yielding 7.5% per year. However, they make a single deposit of $10,000 and make no future contributions to the fund. When Sally is ready to begin college in about 19 years, her fund will have amassed $41,394.60

While both sets of parents put roughly the same amount into the account (actually Billy's parents end up investing a total of $10,700), Sally's parents receive a tremendous benefit from having more money working for them (i.e. working = compounding) at a higher interest rate over a longer period of time. The benefit to Sally equates to approximately 85% more money than Billy when it's time to start college.

Use the greatest mathematical discovery of all times to your advantage. Allow your money to receive the benefit of compounding interest.

MASTERING YOUR MONEY

One of the best ways to master your money is to learn the discipline of contentment. The Apostle Paul spoke of this discipline in his letter to the Philippians, telling them he knew what it meant to be in need and he knew what it meant to have plenty. Regardless of the circumstances, Paul had learned to be content in all situations (Philippians 4:12). He went on to say, "I can do everything through him who gives me strength." (v. 13)

When we recognize that all we have comes from our Creator, we tend to live (and spend) a little differently. It's been said that God can do more with ten percent than we can do with the remaining ninety percent. How true that is. When we pursue Extraordinary Living, we make a conscious decision that earning, spending, saving, or borrowing money will never rule our lives. Instead, we decide to master our money so that we never have to risk being mastered by it. No matter how much we earn, we spend less and we funnel that "unspent" money in wise directions.

THE FOURTH KEY TO EXTRAORDINARY LIVING –
"NO MATTER HOW MUCH YOU EARN, SPEND LESS."

KEY POINTS

- Personal financial management is not a difficult process, but it requires a plan and the discipline to follow that plan.

- The basic fundamentals of personal finance revolve around earning, spending, saving, borrowing and investing.

- An extraordinary life is a financially disciplined life … one in which conscious decision-making occurs with even the most trivial spending.

- Borrowing to purchase expendable items or rapidly depreciating assets using credit cards and bank loans is flirting with a trip to the poorhouse.

- Earning money is not contradictory to God's intention for our lives.

- Money only becomes a problem when we try to serve it rather than master it.

- Mastering our money or being mastered by it is usually determined by the condition of our hearts, not the condition of our back accounts.

- Too many people base their purchases on what they can afford each month rather than the overall value of what they are buying.

- There is one concept about wealth-building that even the most novice investor should know. The concept that has been referred to as "the greatest mathematical discovery of all times" – compound interest.

- When we recognize that all we have comes from our Creator, we tend to live (and spend) a little differently.

- When we spend less than we earn we can funnel unspent money in wise directions.

KEY ACTIONS

- Complete an immediate assessment of your financial condition. Visit our website www.AbundantLifeProject.com and download the blank financial statements/instructions, as well as the "Rapid Debt Reduction" planning guide.

- Once you determine your monthly cash flow and your net worth, take a look at your level of consumer debt (bank & auto loans, credit cards – everything but your mortgage).

- Establish 3-5 financial goals for yourself and/or your family, and put a plan in place to achieve those goals.

CHAPTER SEVEN

The Gift of Giving

"Do all the good you can, by all the means you can, in all the ways you can, in all the places you can, at all the times you can, to all the people you can, as long as you ever can."

John Wesley

A man moved to New England and decided to build a house. Having no idea where to dig his well, he allowed an old-timer to find water with a divining rod. When the old-timer found a water source where the well would be built, he had some advice for the new resident. "You must pump the water each day." As he left, again he warned the resident, "Pump the water each day."

The new resident followed the advice of his seasoned friend and pumped water from the well each day like clock work. What he discovered was that the more he pumped the water in the well the sweeter it became. After a period of time, though, the new owner became lax, forgot about pumping the well and left on a trip. When he returned, there was still water in the well. However, it only lasted two days and then the well went dry. The next time he went to town, he told the old-timer about his dry well. "Did you pump the water every day?" the old-timer asked. He explained that an underground river is fed by thousands of capillaries. As water flows through these capillaries, the power of the river keeps them open, but when the water is not pumped out of the well, the capillaries fill and the river becomes stagnant, causing it to seek another route through the underground. "You lost the river," the old-timer explained, "because you quit using the water."

> *"Money is a great treasure that only increases as you give it away."*
> Sir Francis Bacon

One of the results of the Scarcity Mentality is that in the attempt to hang onto as much as possible we have far less to account for. Just like in this story, when we fail to "pump the well," to use the blessings we have been given to help others, they eventually stop flowing in our direction. The best prescription for a case of the Scarcity Mentality is to become a generous person. The best way to develop or perpetuate a case of scarcity-thinking is to practice hoarding and tightfistedness.

Most people who knew Bertha Adams assumed she was just another welfare victim. However, an autopsy revealed that she had severe malnutrition and poverty was clearly evident throughout her apartment. There was a lack of heat, food, and other basic necessities for living. There could only be one conclusion: Bertha Adams was an obvious example of one who was missed by the national safety net of social spending. At least that was the consensus until the authorities found the

When we fail to use the blessings we've received to bless others, they eventually stop flowing in our direction.

safety deposit box in the local bank. In the box they found almost $800,000 in cash. Also stuffed in this box were hundreds of valuable and negotiable stock certificates, bonds, and other securities. Mrs. Adams had a misguided perspective. Apparently, in her view, earthly possessions were something to be hoarded. She didn't understand that the blessings she had received were given to meet not only her needs, but also the needs of others.

This chapter will teach us that the more we give, the more we are able to live ... really live. In fact, that is the fifth key to unlocking *The Abundance Principle* in our lives.

Give more and you'll live more.

STATISTICS

According to David Bach in his book *Start Late, Finish Rich,* 33 million people do not know where or when they are going to get their next meal. To bring it a little closer to home, 8 million Americans regularly go hungry and 3.5 million Americans have no place to live. Over the next five or six years, the homeless population is expected to double in size. One out of every five human beings on the planet – more than 840 million people – is malnourished, more than 153 million of which are children under the age of five.

According to the Food and Agriculture Organization of the UN, some six million children under the age of five die from hunger and preventable diseases every year. That equates to about 12 children a minute ... every minute ... every single day.

A reality we have to face is that we live in a world where needs abound – the United States included. Another reality is that the government, despite its best effort, apparently cannot nor ever will be able to meet all of the needs we know of let alone those which slip unnoticed, under the radar of common awareness.

While doing an admirable job, non-profit organizations, including churches, have limited resources. We know that organizations such as the Salvation Army and Goodwill do a tremendous job of easing the discomforts of many. We applaud their efforts. However, it seems that where one need is met, two more rise from the dust.

Twelve children die from hunger every single minute of every single day.

On a daily basis, people visit churches and local shelters seeking some form of financial assistance, especially during the days leading up to and throughout the holiday season. Every week many must be turned away. There just aren't enough resources to go around.

THE QUESTIONS OF GIVING

Who will step forward and, from their own resources, begin to answer the call for help? It is our hope that you will join in improving the lives of hundreds and thousands of people. However, one of the first questions that comes to mind when we face a human in need is, "Should we?" Should we do anything at all? Should we get involved? For many, this is where the battle between abundance and scarcity is won or lost.

At one point in the earthly ministry of Jesus, He was preparing to send out His disciples to do the work of ministry. One of the final bits of instruction He gave to them is recorded in Matthew 10.

"And if anyone gives even a cup of cold water to one of these little ones because he is my disciple, I tell you the truth, he will certainly not lose his reward."

Matthew 10:42

Did you catch that? Look at it backwards. Our reward is very definitely related to our activity. Our activity should very much be related to meeting the real needs of human beings. In another place, Jesus clarifies this point further by saying that when we meet such needs, we are doing it unto Him. To the question, "Should we?" The answer is, "Absolutely!"

The next obvious question we tend to face is, "How do we help?" Or, "What do we do?" Let's just keep the answer simple: Everyone should do what they can. That seems fair enough. But is there level ground where we all begin – a starting line of sorts where we can begin giving to make a difference?

The beginning point of giving is commonly referred to as a tithe.

> *"We make a living by what we get, we make a life by what we give."*
> Winston Churchill

In its basic definition, tithe means a tenth. Each of us should set a minimum goal of giving away a tenth of our income. While tithing is essentially a biblical concept, a person does not have to be a religious person to tithe. It can simply represent the concept of investing into others what has been invested in us. In fact, it might do us good if we view all of our blessings as the seeds of which we should take a portion and plant into the lives of others. This planting seeds of blessing in others, financially or otherwise, is perhaps one of the greatest joys of extraordinary living.

God even gave us permission to put him to the test in this regard.

He said, "Try me." The prophet Malachi confirms this statement in the following passage:

"Bring the whole tithe into the storehouse, that there may be food in my house. Test me in this, says the Lord Almighty, and see if I will not throw open the floodgates of Heaven and pour out so much blessing that you will not have room enough for it."

Malachi 3:10

Of course the opposite would be true as well. The way to live a pauper's life (and we don't just mean it in the financial sense) is to hoard what we have and never give anything away. This is a spiritual principle which is clearly articulated in the Bible.

Here is just a sampling:

"A generous man will himself be blessed, for he shares his food with the poor."

Proverbs 22:9

"He who gives to the poor will lack nothing, but he who closes his eyes to them receives many curses."

Proverbs 28:27

"One man gives freely, yet gains even more; another withholds unduly, but comes to poverty. A generous man will prosper; he who refreshes others will himself be refreshed."

Proverbs 11: 24-25

SOLOMON'S EXAMPLE

As we can see, the idea of "giving more leads to living more" is not a new concept. As our scriptures indicate, the wisest and wealthiest man in the world – and the writer of Proverbs – King Solomon, understood it well. In fact, his path to wealth was a result of a giving mindset.

At the beginning of King Solomon's rule, God asked him a question which is recorded in 1 Kings. Basically, God gave Solomon the opportunity to ask for whatever he wanted. Think of the power of this moment. Solomon had the opportunity to ask the Creator of the universe for anything. What he asked for was nothing short of amazing. He didn't ask for riches, or beautiful women, or power, or victory in battle. Solomon asked for one thing and one thing only. He asked for wisdom.

A bank full of money is no guarantee we'll live abundant lives.

Solomon's response to God's question has three powerful lessons to teach us about giving more and living more. The first lesson is subtle but no less powerful than those which follow:

- **Solomon's choice was a privilege handed down from his father** – If you are a parent, this should give you pause. Listen to Solomon's humble words to God:

"Solomon answered, You have shown great kindness to your servant, my father David, because he was faithful to you and righteous and upright in heart. You have continued this great kindness to him and have given him a son to sit on his throne this very day."

1 Kings 3:6

Notice that Solomon's understanding of who he was, where he came from, and the decision he was about to make was directly related to the faithfulness of his father, King David, who instilled the values that were about ready to drive Solomon's decision.

As parents we have the awesome privilege and tremendous responsibility to transfer into our children the wonderful benefits of **The Abundance Principle.** One of the best ways to invest hope and opportunity into the future is to teach our kids to give. The reality is that if we are seen by our children as generous, they will most likely end up being generous as well.

- **Solomon chose to ask for something he could give away** –
  Solomon essentially wanted a gift that he could give away every time he was faced with making a decision regarding the lives of the people for whom he was responsible. And he would eventually do that again and again. Was it a monetary gift? No. Was it a tithe? No. Could it be banked? Not in a literal sense. Yet in the long run Solomon was asking for something that he could bestow on another person in order to bring a just result.

What would change in our lives if everything we received, whether a pay check, profits from an investment, a Christmas bonus, a particular talent or an educational degree was viewed as an opportunity to give back rather than store up?

- **Solomon chose to receive what would benefit others** – There is a nugget of truth here we must not overlook. Upon whom did Solomon want to bestow his wisdom? Obviously the people he was charged with leading. No less than four times Solomon says the word "people" within the framework of verses 8 and 9 in

1 Kings 3. Solomon's interest in having wisdom was to improve the lives of people through his discerning judgments as their King.

There can be nothing more valuable in life than the people around us. As you have already read, one of the keys to **The Abundance Principle** guides us to invest strongly in relationships. We need each other. Everything we do affects the well-being of those around us ... hopefully for the better.

In the same way, our interest in having more of anything is so that we can give more. People ought to be our first priority. Unfortunately, sometimes others are the last thing on our minds.

If you have ever been a server in a restaurant you know how demanding and uncaring some people can be. In fact, the next time you are in a restaurant, ask your server which day of the week has the worst crowd to deal with and who that crowd represents. The server will most likely tell you Sunday is the worst day to work because the church crowd tends to be the most difficult. Unfortunately, we've probably all witnessed church people, standing in crowded after-worship lunch lines in local restaurants treat their servers badly because their service was slow or the orders were wrong. Dressed in their Sunday Best, they punctuate their poor behavior by leaving only a paltry tip. Many restaurant workers hate to work on Sundays because the church crowd tends to be more difficult, less forgiving, and the stingiest of all their patrons.

Most restaurant servers will tell you the worst day of the week to work is Sunday because the church crowd tends to be more difficult, less forgiving, and less generous than all other customers.

133

Isn't it interesting that the group which should be the most generous is often times the cheapest? Why is that? Perhaps the Scarcity Mentality is once again at work. Perhaps restaurant behavior is a good indicator of a person's abundance quotient. In fact, how generous a person really is can often be determined by how he tips after a meal and how he treats those in vocations or professions of service.

What was the result of Solomon's request for wisdom? God was so impressed with Solomon's "give first" mentality, that He honored his request and gave Solomon such a gift of wisdom that …

"…there will never have been anyone like you, nor will there ever be".
1 Kings 3:12

From this we are led to believe that there has never been, nor will there ever be anyone as wise as Solomon. But the story doesn't end there. The residual effect of Solomon's abundance mentality is that God gave him everything he could have asked for but didn't.

"Moreover, I will give you what you have not asked for--
both riches and honor--so that in your lifetime you will have
no equal among kings."
1 Kings 3:13

Solomon's choice to put others' needs before his own provides two powerful lessons for us:

1. **His choice brought him untold wealth**
2. **His choice brought honor and respect**

Here we see that the definite result of Solomon's "give more" mentality was that he experienced a "live more" life – apparently more than anyone in the history of mankind.

The idea of living more through giving more is as old as the ancient words of scripture. In Chapter 1, we related the "Parable of the Rich Fool." Reread the words of Jesus as recorded in Luke 12:

"And he told them this parable: The ground of a certain rich man produced a good crop. He thought to himself, What shall I do? I have no place to store my crops. Then he said, This is what I'll do. I will tear down my barns and build bigger ones, and there I will store all my grain and my goods. And I'll say to myself, "You have plenty of good things laid up for many years. Take life easy; eat, drink and be merry."" "But God said to him, 'You fool! This very night your life will be demanded from you. Then who will get what you have prepared for yourself?' "This is how it will be with anyone who stores up things for himself but is not rich toward God."

Luke 12: 16-21

We can see that the scarcity mindset that leads to hoarding is really an empty hope. It just doesn't work. A bank full of money is no guarantee that we will live lives of abundance. In fact, the above Scripture teaches that if we have much, but are not doing anything with it, we will eventually end up with nothing. The wisdom writer in Ecclesiastes confirms that for us:

"I have seen a grievous evil under the sun: wealth hoarded to the harm of its owner."

Ecclesiastes 5:13

PERSONAL EXPERIENCE

I (Jeff) have to confess that giving has not always come easily for me. In fact, it's been a struggle most of my life. Growing up, I lived a good, middle-class lifestyle with a wonderful family. One thing my parents taught me was the value of hard work. So much so, that I have worked extremely hard my entire life, beginning in the fifth grade mowing yards, continuing through high school where I worked at a local gas station. Upon graduation from high school, I entered Army Basic Training. Throughout college, I worked full-time as an emergency medical technician, paramedic, and respiratory therapist. Money was always something I worked very hard for and when you work that hard for something, you don't tend to loosen your grip very easily. Little did I know the blessings that would await me once I learned how to give more freely.

Early in my marriage, I began writing a check to our church on a weekly basis. However, as I would begin filling in the amount, an imaginary noose would tighten around my neck and I could almost literally find it difficult to breathe. It didn't happen every time, but it happened frequently enough that I knew I had to get a handle on it.

At one point, I decided that every time I felt the "scarcity noose" tighten around my neck, I would force myself to write the check for $50 more than I had planned. It was a difficult battle, but as I followed through with that commitment, I found the noose tightening episodes occurred less and less. I also noticed that my income began to grow, and soon I was writing the checks to the church for more and more, and feeling less and less pressure or negativity for doing so.

I'm not sure when the final change came, but sometime approximately 10-12 years after I had begun that simple practice, I

> "What I kept I lost, what I spent I had, what I gave I have."
> Persian Proverb

realized that giving was a true joy. I began looking for ways to help out financially. Now don't get me wrong, that old ugly noose shows up now and again. However, those instances are few and far between. And, no matter how tight it gets, I'm going to keep giving.

ATTITUDE CHECK

Giving doesn't always come naturally to everyone. We've already talked about how a $20-bill looks so small at the grocery store and so large when the offering plate passes in front of us. Author and motivational expert Zig Ziglar suggests that some folks may have some negative attitudes about giving to overcome.

- **"Some will say, 'I'm in debt, I can't give.'"**

Many people feel they are too broke to give. But think about it. It was wrong thinking that got them into debt. Continued wrong thinking about giving will keep them in debt. What will get them out of debt? Right thinking … Right thinking about giving and then right thinking about managing what's left.

- **"Some will say, 'I'll give more when I get more.'"**

The problem with this approach is that generally more money doesn't change anything. Only a change in the way we think will create more money. Just as wrong thinking will keep a person from having more money, it will also keep people from giving more money.

- **"Some will say, 'I can't give.' "**

This is the attitude that plays the blame game. It's the bosses fault or my circumstances or the economy. But let's ask some questions before we point the finger. Are you in debt because of downsizing or because of the new car you just purchased? Is it the economy or is it the vacation you paid for with your credit card? The reality is that some people pay for their own poverty. Usually it is poverty of attitude that is the main culprit.

> *"You can't help the poor by being one of them."*
> Abraham Lincoln

- **"Some will say, 'I won't give. I'm mad!' "**

Usually some sort of bitterness is behind this statement. Bitterness sucks the joy right out of our lives and it shows up in our attitudes. James the apostle asked a good question:

"What causes fights and quarrels among you? Don't they come from your desires that battle within you? You want something but don't get it. You kill and covet, but you cannot have what you want. You quarrel and fight. You do not have, because you do not ask God."

James 4:1-2

- **"Some will say, 'I'm not giving. I'm giving up!' "**

Some folks just decide to throw in the towel. They stop caring. Everyone and everything is out to get them.

HOW DO YOU RATE?

Here is a little test to determine where you actually fall in regards to generosity. The four statements below represent four attitudes of giving. Rate yourself on a scale of 1-5. One would be totally false. Five would be very true. Where do you find yourself? Be honest.

Statement	Description
1. I have to give.	This is the unenthusiastic giver who does so, but is really saying, "If I didn't have to, I wouldn't."
2. I need to give.	Giving in this mindset is only activated when our conscience meets an opportunity. In other words, we will only give if we see someone or something that needs our attention. Then we close ourselves to generosity until the next guilt trip comes along. "I need to but please don't ask."
3. I want to give.	This kind of giver would love nothing more than giving, they just never follow through – or maybe they think the only thing to give is money and since money is short, there is nothing to give. "I want to give but I have nothing to offer."
4. I get to give.	This person loves to give gifts of all kinds and does so regularly. From giving of themselves, to giving money, to buying something in the store for a friend just because the other person "would love this."

The scriptures are clear about the key to prosperity. It is not accumulated wealth that determines a person's real net worth, it's actually dispersed wealth. We are told by Jesus that the way to accumulate wealth is to give it away. It doesn't seem to make sense does it? But there it is in bold letters:

"Give and it will be given to you."

Luke 6: 38

Talk about a shift of mindset. This certainly is not the generally accepted standard of those who are on a quest to possess more of the earth's treasures. For some, giving is just not an option. It is a concept some people simply cannot understand.

LEARNING TO GIVE

So how does one become a giving person? Where does it really begin. Without question generosity starts with a choice. It begins in the mind. If our minds do not accept it, our pocketbooks will not project it.

When it comes to developing a right attitude toward giving, neither your own belief about money, nor your belief about those who have or those who do not have money are most important. The most important thing is your mindset.

One of the greatest examples comes from the life of a man in the Old Testament. His name was Job. He was wealthy by any standard. In one day he lost his livelihood, his children were killed, and his property was destroyed. Any bad day we've ever had pales in comparison to this guy's bad day. What we want you to see though, are his words in the first chapter of Job. When the dust of the day settled, this is what he said:

"Naked I came from my mother's womb, and naked I will depart. The LORD gave and the LORD has taken away; may the name of the LORD be praised."

Job 1:21

What a great example of an abundant disposition. Job knew all he had came from God and he was completely faithful, even in the face of total material devastation.

> *"Giving does not begin with a donation – it begins with a disposition."*
> Stan Toler

When we understand God's view of economics, it changes the way we think about money and what we do with our money. In God's economy we receive in order that we might give it away. In fact, if you really want to live more, you have to give more. The more you give, the more you live. Jesus articulated these words in Luke 6:

"Give and it will be given to you. A good measure, pressed down, shaken together and running over, will be poured into your lap. For with the measure you use, it will be measured to you."

Luke 6:38

Did you catch that? For with the measure you use, it will be measured to you. The degree to which you give, is the degree to which you will live. Only in God's economy can we be guaranteed a return on our investment. What we give comes back to us, because God openly rewards giving. When God's wealth flows into the lives of believers, He intends for it to be shared with others. Again, the degree to which you give, is the degree to which you will live.

If you give cheaply you will live cheaply in all aspects of life. If you give modestly, you will live modestly. If you give generously, you will live generously. And just so you don't think we're making this up, Jesus Himself said:

> *"Remember this: Whoever sows sparingly will also reap sparingly, and whoever sows generously will also reap generously."*
>
> 2 Corinthians 9:6

Sadly, too much of today's theology of stewardship suggests that giving is a mechanism to getting. That philosophy suggests, "If you really want to prosper, then here's how you do it." The motivation for giving becomes getting something in return. In reality, giving is primary ... getting is secondary and not the other way around.

The fact of the matter is that God will bless our giving. Sometimes he blesses it with financial increase. Sometimes the blessing comes in the form of a deep, heartfelt joy. Sometimes the blessing manifests itself in more intangible ways, such as happiness and contentment.

Regardless of the manner in which God chooses to bless our giving, ultimately His blessing is not for our benefit alone. He blesses us so that we might bless others, which in turn causes us to be blessed even more, so that we might be more of a blessing to others. When we get into that cycle of giving and living, life is exciting.

DELIGHT IN GIVING

A recently published article tells the story about a church who loved to give. In fact, every Sunday when the pastor invited the ushers to come forward to receive the morning offering, the congregation broke out into spontaneous applause. Now that's a different mindset. The Bible says that God loves a cheerful giver. One of the critical dispositions of generosity is delight. This church took that concept literally. They delighted in their giving.

The measure of a person's net worth is not determined by the weight of his gold but by the generosity of his spirit.

We want to make it clear that as we have discussed the aspects of giving more in order to live more, we have not been referring only to the giving of money. Money is often the most "tangible" gift, but it's not always the "best" gift. There are many ways to give. In the tenth chapter of Matthew, Jesus tells the disciples:

"… heal the sick, raise the dead, cleanse those who have leprosy, drive out demons. Freely you have received, freely give."

Matthew 10:8

One of the best gifts we can offer is the gift of ourselves. The following suggestions are ways you can make yourself available to others:

- Write a letter of encouragement to someone who's discouraged;

- Spend an hour with an old friend, and say how much you appreciate him or her;

- Hug a member of your family, and say why you love him or her;

- Visit someone in the hospital, and pray a prayer of faith;

- Give the gift of kindness to someone who needs help;

- Spend some time in a nursing home encouraging the residents;

- Volunteer your time in a local charity;

- Offer to babysit the children of a single parent;

Use your own special abilities or talents to help someone who might not ever know what you've done;

STILL NOT CONVINCED?

"Imagine this," Lee Strobel wrote in *God's Outrageous Claims,* "Our omniscient God sees every act of service motivated by His love, every instance of giving to build his kingdom, every sacrifice in His name, and He solemnly promises to reward us in eternity … He even remembers our acts of kindness that we ourselves have forgotten." The serious question we must ask ourselves is this – What will He recall about me? If generosity were a crime, would there be enough evidence to convict me?

> *"I do not believe one can settle how much we ought to give. I am afraid the only safe rule is to give more than we can spare."*
> C.S. Lewis

Todd Beamer showed an act of selfless courage on September 11, 2001. Trapped on a flight where terrorists had killed the pilot and commandeered the cockpit, he realized he was about to die. He used the in-flight phone to call his home. Unable to reach his wife, he prayed the Lord's Prayer with the Airfone operator as a testimony to his faith. After saying "good-bye," he turned and uttered the words, "Let's roll." The rest, as they say, is history.

There is a story about a wealthy fellow who took a detailed inventory of his personal belongings every year. Upon reviewing the listing of his possessions, he would retrieve his most prized possession from the list. After spending a little time with the treasure, making certain

> *"If you give what you do not need, it isn't giving."*
> Mother Theresa

it was in fact, his most prized treasure, he would then proceed to give it away. He articulated his purpose for doing so, "If I am able to give away my most prized possession, then I truly own it. If I am unable to give it away, it owns me."

If generosity were a crime, would there be enough evidence to convict you?

The poignancy of that story certainly hits home. When we realize that giving does not rob us of anything but actually generates both tangible and intangible increase in our lives, we start to live in a totally different way. When we make the giant leap from having the attitude that says, "What must I give?" to the attitude that says, "What can I give?" life takes on a whole new meaning. This leap doesn't happen over night. It happens because we choose to start giving more … and in the process, we start living more!

THE FIFTH KEY TO EXTRAORDINARY LIVING –
"GIVE MORE AND YOU'LL LIVE MORE"

KEY POINTS

- One of the causes of the Scarcity Mentality is that in the attempt to hang on to as much as possible, we end up having far less to account for. When we fail to use what we have been given to help others, blessing eventually stops flowing in our direction.

- Government, apparently cannot, nor ever will be able to meet all of the needs of our country.

- For many, the battle between abundance and scarcity is often won or lost in whether or not we get involved in meeting needs around us.

- The next obvious question is, "How do we help?" The answer is simple: The beginning point should be giving away a tithe, or a tenth of our income.

- Planting seeds of blessing in others, financially or otherwise, is perhaps one of the greatest joys of extraordinary living.

- Modeling a generous spirit in front of our children teaches them to be generous themselves.

- Our interest in having more is so that we can give more. People ought to be our first priority. Unfortunately, the last thing on our minds, sometimes, is people.

- We've seen that the scarcity mindset that leads to hoarding is really an empty hope. Scriptures declare that if we have much, but are not doing anything with it, we will eventually end up with nothing.

- The Scriptures are clear about the key to prosperity. It is not "accumulated wealth" that determines a person's real net worth. The indicator is actually "dispersed wealth." In fact, we are told by Jesus that the way to accumulate wealth is to give it away.

- When we realize that giving does not rob us of anything, but actually generates increase in our lives, we start to live in a totally different way. When we move from the attitude that says, "What must I give?" to the attitude that says, "What can I give?" life takes on a whole new meaning. We start giving more, and in the process, we start living more.

KEY ACTIONS

- Calculate a "tithe" or a tenth of your income (10%). After calculating that number, compare it to your current level of giving. If you're not quite there, set a personal goal to take a step toward tithing each year.

- Using the Internet or a traditional Bible concordance, locate and read as many Scripture passages as you can find about tithing, giving, and serving. Identify your favorite passages, making notes about how they apply to your life.

- Take a sheet of paper and inventory your personal feelings about giving. Be honest with yourself. Is giving a struggle, a necessary evil, or a joy? Spend time contemplating how you will move toward "the joy of giving."

- Consider setting aside a special "fund" of money to which you contribute a small amount each month, that will be used solely to respond to the needs of others in crisis.

- List three people who could significantly benefit from your assistance. Below each name, detail exactly how you will assist them over the next 30 days. Follow through on your plans.

CHAPTER EIGHT

Resolving to Live Extraordinarily

"The world makes way for a man who knows where he's going."
Ralph Waldo Emerson

In the Canadian Northlands only two seasons are experienced each year – winter and July. As the roads begin to thaw leading up to and during the month of July, they become very muddy. As with all muddy roads, vehicles traveling at this time leave deep ruts. As the winter again comes around, the ground freezes hard making the ruts a significant obstacle to travelers. Near one particular area where deep ruts normally develop, there is reportedly a sign which reads, "Drivers, please choose carefully which rut you drive in. You'll be in it for the next 20 miles." So it is with life. We must choose carefully the paths we take in our lives, as we will become who we are tomorrow, because of the choices we make today.

You've now been introduced to one of the most life-changing principles known to man ... **The Abundance Principle.** In addition, we've given you five very specific keys to unlock the treasure trove of this tremendous principle in your life starting today. You have

> *"You don't have to be great to get started, but you have to get started to be great."*
> Zig Ziglar

everything you need to get started. But getting started is something you must do. Wayne Gretzky, world renowned hockey player once said, "You'll miss 100% of the shots you never take." Now is the time to plan and take your shot at Extraordinary Living.

Earlier, we discussed Napoleon Hill, the protégé of Andrew Carnegie who spent 20 plus years defining the traits and characteristics of highly successful people. Among other findings from Hill's research were that these successful people all used the following principles and practices to fuel their success:

- They used applied faith, the art of believing by doing, to get where they wanted to go;

- They created personal initiative to get the ball rolling and keep it rolling in the right direction(s);

- They controlled their attention … they focused on the objective or end result;

- They enforced self-discipline and tenacious persistence until they achieved that which they sought.

In the second chapter of James, we are told that "faith by itself, if it is not accompanied by action, is dead." The author James goes on to explain that our faith and our action work together to produce specific results and that our faith is made complete by the actions we choose to take.

So, what's stopping you from taking action right now? What's stopping you from using the applied faith that Napoleon Hill found was a critical success factor for all of those he studied? To repeat the words of Thomas Edison, "Seeming to do is not doing."

Hopefully up to this point, you've carried out the Key Actions located at the end of each chapter. If you haven't, we highly recommend you put a plan in place to do that immediately. You'll be glad you did.

OVERCOMING THE OBSTACLES

There are a number of obstacles, distractions, and hindrances that will inevitably try to get in the way of Extraordinary Living. Knowing about these obstacles on the front-end and then doing what is necessary to

> *"The people who get ahead in this world are the people who get up and look for the circumstances they want, and if they can't find them, make them."*
> George Bernard Shaw

prevent or overcome them when they do appear will be critical to your success.

- **Procrastination** – We've talked "around" this one already. The bottom line is, don't do it! Create a plan and take action to move in the direction you want. Don't wait for motivation. Motivation follows thoughtful action. Abraham Lincoln is credited with saying, "Leave nothing for tomorrow which can be done today." So it is with extraordinary living. Just do it!

- **Worry** – It's been said that worry gives a small thing a very big shadow. Most often, that which we worry about never comes to pass. Probably the most useless mental activity available to us is that of worry. It serves no worthwhile purpose and it robs us today of the joy we could be experiencing. Put your applied faith into action and you won't have time for useless worry.

- **Selfishness** – It's so easy to get caught up in our own selfish motives and intentions. The remedy to this obstacle is an appropriate focus on the Fifth Key to Extraordinary Living – "Give more and you'll live more." Proactive giving and serving is the best way to prevent the development of a self-centered disposition. However, selfishness is a very subtle obstacle and we must be on guard against it continuously.

- **Isolation** – Relationships are vital to success no matter the endeavor. The good thing about the journey to extraordinary living is that you don't have to do it alone. The fact is trying to do it alone is a potential obstacle in and of itself. We recommend that you find a few family members, co-workers, or close friends and invite them to take this journey with you. A great way to start a journey like this is with the help of an accountability group – a small group of 2-3 people with whom you have a fairly close relationship and to whom you can submit yourself for inspection. Ken Blanchard once said, "You can expect what you inspect." By submitting yourself to regular "inspection" by a group of close friends, you greatly increase the likelihood Extraordinary Living will take root in your life.

Once you identify this group of "inspectors," you may visit The Abundant Life Project website (www.AbundantLifeProject.com) to download a Study Guide for use in your weekly, monthly or other periodic sessions together.

EIGHT WEEKS TO EXTRAORDINARY LIVING

Research into the psychology of habit formation indicates that it takes about 21 days to break an old habit by replacing it with a new one. Most of us fail in our efforts to change habits because we don't know how or where to begin. Moving from wanting to doing is a critical step in the process. Continuing to "do" for a period of 21 to 30 days will dramatically increase the likelihood that your new activities will become constructive, new habits.

We've developed an "Action Plan" to help you formulate the new habits that will move you in the direction you desire. Whether you begin this journey on your own or you enlist the support of an "inspection team" as we recommend, the following plan should help you begin moving in the right direction.

- Identify a period of eight weeks where you can spend 30 minutes or so each day (about 3-5 hours each week) focused on the content presented in this book and supporting materials.

- Establish a formal starting date for when you will launch this personal and/or group study.

- If you chose to establish a study group or inspection team to take the journey with you, enlist that team and agree on a starting date as well as meeting times and requirements.

- Download the Study Guide from www.AbundantLifeProject.com.

- Take a few moments to identify every person, place, or thing for which you are grateful and write them all down in a place where you can review them daily for the next eight weeks. If you did this after reading Chapter 2, then revisit and update this list if necessary.

- At least once every day for the entire eight weeks of your study period, spend a few moments expressing your gratitude to God for these wonderful blessings in your life. Review and add to your list as you do this, being certain to cultivate true feelings of gratitude.

- In addition to your daily dose of gratitude, spend one week focused on each of the following sections from this book, as well as the additional Study Guide information:
    - Week One – The Scarcity Mentality
    - Week Two – The Abundance Mentality
    - Week Three – Master your thoughts and change your life.
    - Week Four – Plan your life and live your passion.
    - Week Five – Build and maintain strong relationships.
    - Week Six – No matter how much you earn, spend less.
    - Week Seven – Give more and you'll live more.
    - Week Eight – Wrap-up and Planning for the Future

We are delighted you've chosen to spend this time with us exploring **The Abundance Principle.** We believe God has given us this message to share and are honored to have the opportunity to share it with you and with others.   Remember … An abundant life has been God's plan for you from the very beginning. Take action now to pursue that life with a vengeance. You'll be glad you did, so will we … and so will God!

"And now to Him who is able to do exceeding abundantly more than we can even think or ask through the power that works within you …"
Ephesians 3: 20-21 (NKJV)

Grace and Peace to you.

ABOUT THE AUTHORS

Dr. Jeff D. Standridge – currently holds a senior leadership position for a publicly-traded, multinational technology company headquartered in Little Rock, Arkansas. Formerly, he was a professor in the University of Arkansas System and still maintains active involvement with a number of educational institutions. He has been the recipient of numerous professional awards and special recognition, including being recognized in 2004 by Arkansas Business Magazine as one of the Top 40 Business Leaders under 40 years of age. He is retired from the U.S. Army-Arkansas Army National Guard. Dr. Standridge holds the Doctor of Education degree with special work in Adult Learning, Organizational and Leadership Development, and Teaching. He has been an invited speaker, trainer, and consultant for numerous businesses, organizations, and institutions of higher education across the U.S., Canada and Europe. He resides in Conway, Arkansas with his wife Lori and their two daughters Katie and Anna. They are active members of Conway First United Methodist Church.

Rev. Tim Kellerman – is Lead Pastor at the First Church of the Nazarene in Conway, Arkansas where he has served for 10 years. He holds a Bachelor of Arts degree in Theology and is currently pursuing a Master of Arts degree in Pastoral Ministry with an emphasis in Church Management. Additionally, he is a graduate of the School of Large Church Management. Tim's formative years were in Taiwan where his parents served as missionaries for 17 years. Tim is a certified Search and Rescue Scuba Diver, has attained a brown-belt ranking in TaeKwon-Do, and is an avid Racquetball player. He resides in Conway, Arkansas with his wife Jamie, daughter Sarah and son Seth.

Jeff and Tim are both co-Founders of The Abundant Life Project™. Together they bring a unique blend of perspectives and insight, drawing on their personal experiences in business, organizational leadership, academic research, and pastoral ministry.

SUGGESTED READING AND FURTHER RESEARCH

KEY ONE: MASTER YOUR THOUGHTS AND CHANGE YOUR LIFE:

Allen, James. *As a Man Thinketh*. New York: NY, GP Putnam's Sons.

Harrell, Keith. *Attitude is Everything: 10 Life-changing Steps to Turning Attitude into Action*. New York, NY: HarperCollins. 2002.

Frankl, Viktor E. *Man's Search for Meaning*. London: UK. Rider (Random House). 1959 (2004).

Maxwell, John C. *Attitude 101: What Every Leader Needs to Know*. Nashville, TN: T. Nelson. 2003.

Osteen, Joel. *Your Best Life Now: 7 Steps to Living at your Full Potential*. New York, NY: Warner Faith. 2005.

Seamands, David. *Putting Away Childish Things*. Wheaton, Illinois: Victor Books. 1982.

Schuller, Robert. *The Be Happy Attitudes: Eight Positive Attitudes that can Transform Your Life*. Waco, Texas: Word Books. 1985.

KEY TWO: PLAN YOUR LIFE AND LIVE YOUR PASSION

Canfield, Jack. *The Success Principles*. New York, NY: HarperCollins. 2005.

Covey, Stephen R. *Seven Habits of Highly Effective People*. New York, NY: Simon and Schuster. 1989.

Covey, Stephen, R. *Living the 7 Habits: The Courage to Change*. London, UK: Simon and Schuster. 1999.

Gore, Gary W. *Navigating Change: A Field Guide to Personal Growth.* Memphis, TN: TeamTrek. 2002

Lucado, Max. *Cure for the Common Life: Living in Your Sweet Spot.* Nashville, TN: W. Publishing Group. 2005.

Maxwell, John C. *Your Roadmap for Success.* Nashville, TN: T. Nelson. 2002.

Warren, Rick. *The Purpose Driven Church.* Grand Rapids: Zondervan Publishing. 1995.

KEY THREE: BUILD AND MAINTAIN STRONG RELATIONSHIPS

Byock, Ira. *The Four Things that Matter Most: A Book About Living.* New York, NY: Free Press. 2004.

Dobson, James C. *Dare To Discipline.* Wheaton, IL: Tyndale House Publishers. 1970.

Harley, Willard F. *His Needs Her Needs.* Old Tappan, NJ: Revell. 1986.

Omartian, Stormie. *The Power of a Praying Husband.* Eugene, OR: Harvest House. 2001.

Omartian, Stormie. *The Power of a Praying Parent.* Eugene, OR: Harvest House Publishers. 1995.

Omartian, Stormie. *The Power of a Praying Wife.* Eugene, OR: Harvest Publications, Inc. 1997.

Toler, Stan. *The Secret Blend.* Colorado Springs, CO: Waterbrook Press. 2004.

KEY FOUR: NO MATTER HOW MUCH YOU EARN, SPEND LESS

Blue, Ron and Judy. *Money Matters for Parents and Their Kids.*
Nashville, TN: Oliver Nelson. 1988.

Burkett, Larry. *How to Manage Your Money.* Chicago, IL: Moody
Press. 2000.

Dugdale, Bradley, Jr. and Ferrell, Donald M. *Let's Save America: 9
Lessons to Financial Success.* Hayden, ID: Denali Publishing. 2000.

Ramsey, Dave. *Financial Peace.* New York, New York: Penguin
Viking. 1997.

Ramsey, Dave. *The Total Money Makeover.* Nashville, TN: Thomas
Nelson. 2003.

KEY FIVE: GIVE MORE AND YOU'LL LIVE MORE

Chappelear, Jim. *The Daily Six: Six Simple Steps to Find the
Balance of Prosperity and Purpose.* New York, NY: GP Putnam's
Sons. 2005.

Diefendorf, Monroe M. Jr., and Madden, Robert Sterling.
*3 Dimensional Wealth: A Radically Sane Perspective on Wealth
Management.* Locust Valley, NY: 3 Dimensional Wealth Publishing.
2005.

Davidson, Jim. *Learning, Earning, & Giving Back.* Conway, AR:
Continuing Education Services, Inc. 2003.

ABOUT THE ABUNDANT LIFE PROJECT™

MISSION STATEMENT

The Abundant Life Project™ is a ministry of encouragement that transforms the lives of individuals, families, and organizations by helping people develop an active faith. When we put "arms and legs" on our faith and take positive action, miracles happen.

Our goal is that everyone who comes into contact with the Abundant Life Project™ will develop a desire to cultivate hope, healing, & Extraordinary Living around the world. To achieve this goal we must change thousands of lives, but we must do so one life at a time.

The Abundant Life Project™ fulfills its mission through publishing, coaching, training & speaking. To contact us about any of our coaching, training or speaking programs, please visit us at www.AbundantLifeProject.com.

ABUNDANT GIVING

A portion of all proceeds generated through the Abundant Life Project™ will be used to support organizations, ministries and programs that cultivate hope, healing & Extraordinary Living around the world. It is our goal to raise and/or contribute $1,000,000 to these causes within the next decade. To inquire about possible partnerships in this regard, please email us at Partners@AbundantLifeProject.com.

We want to hear from you ...

If you ...

- Have specific questions or feedback about *The Abundance Principle* or The Abundant Life Project;™

- Have specific stories or testimonies about how your life has changed because of this ministry;

- Wish to inquire about special discounts for bulk purchases of *The Abundance Principle: Five Keys to Extraordinary Living;*

- Wish to inquire about speaking and coaching programs or to discuss bringing The Abundant Life Project™ to your church, club, or organization;

Please contact us at the following:

> **The Abundant Life Project**
> 813 Oak Street, Suite 10A-310
> Conway, AR 72032
> Jeff@AbundantLifeProject.com
> Tim@AbundantLifeProject.com

Websites: www.AbundantLifeProject.com
www.TheAbundancePrinciple.com

The Abundance Principle™
An Abundant Life has been God's plan for us from the very beginning.

Five Keys to Extraordinary Living

Master your thoughts and change your life.

Plan your life and live your passion.

Build and maintain strong relationships.

No matter how much you earn, spend less.

Give more and you'll live more!

To Order Additional Copies of
The Abundance Principle: Five Keys to Extraordinary Living
Check your favorite bookstore or order here

YES, I want _____ copies of The Abundance Principle at $15.99 each, plus $5 shipping and handling per book. Non- US orders must be accompanied by a postal money order in U.S. Funds. Please allow 15 days for delivery.

My check or money order for $ _____ is enclosed.
Please make your checks payable and return to:

The Abundant Life Project
813 Oak Street, Suite 10A-310
Conway, AR 72032

Please charge my Credit Card (Check One).
Visa ❏   MasterCard ❏   American Express ❏

Name: _____

Organization : _____

Address: _____

City/State/Zip _____

Phone: _____   Email: _____

Credit Card # _____   Exp. Date _____

Signature _____

For quantity discounts, contact us by email at
Info@AbundantLifeProject.com.
www.AbundantLifeProject.com

To Order Additional Copies of
The Abundance Principle: Five Keys to Extraordinary Living
Check your favorite bookstore or order here

YES, I want _____ copies of The Abundance Principle at $15.99 each, plus $5 shipping and handling per book. Non- US orders must be accompanied by a postal money order in U.S. Funds. Please allow 15 days for delivery.

My check or money order for $ _____ is enclosed. Please make your checks payable and return to:

The Abundant Life Project
813 Oak Street, Suite 10A-310
Conway, AR 72032

Please charge my Credit Card (Check One).
Visa ❏   MasterCard ❏   American Express ❏

Name: _____

Organization : _____

Address: _____

City/State/Zip _____

Phone: _____   Email: _____

Credit Card # _____   Exp. Date _____

Signature _____

For quantity discounts, contact us by email at
Info@AbundantLifeProject.com.
www.AbundantLifeProject.com